Sojourner

in

Ataquay

Sojourner
in
Ataquay

Mind-Expanding Ideas and Practical Tools for the Open-Minded Seeker of a Meaningful Life

Carrie Hart

Systematique, Inc.

Published by Systematique, Inc.
For information, please email Publisher@Systematique.org

Printed in the United States

ISBN: 978-0-9665931-7-4

For Ed, the love of my life

MESSAGE TO READERS

This book is interactive! I am thrilled to show you how to bring it to life. Scan the Quick Response (QR) Codes throughout the book with your Smartphone or SmartDevice to follow the links.

How to Scan the QR Codes in this book:

Step 1: Tap on your camera app to open it on your SmartDevice as if you were going to take a picture.

Step 2: Point your camera at the QR Code you wish to scan. You do not need to take a picture of the QR Code. The camera will automatically scan the QR Code and direct your phone to the appropriate web page that contains each video message from my book.

Try it right now to watch this video I created for you:

Ataquay

(AH'-tuh-kway)

In the Wanataquay language, Ataquay is a place of expanded and shared consciousness, an energetic field beyond ordinary time and space, where everything that is, was and will be exists in a state of pregnant possibility. Ataquay is the mysterious land we visit with our intuition and in our dreams, where serendipity and coincidence are the norm and profound guidance is ours for the taking.

Table of Contents

1 Introduction

Ed always made me laugh.

We met at work in downtown Los Angeles, where I had just started a new job as a computer programmer at the Pacific Stock Exchange. We had a Cute Meet, as they do in romantic comedies. This was in the days when computers used punched cards. Well, Ed came charging into the computer room to solve some crisis, took my huge card deck out of the hopper and accidentally dropped it, scattering my cards across the floor.

That was our very first meeting. Luckily, he knew how to operate the card sorter—you know, like what they used in that old TV show, "The Sixty-Four Thousand Dollar Question."

But I first seriously noticed Ed when we were all sitting in the coffee room with our coworkers. They were talking about their dogs. Someone said, “Ed, you have a Labrador Retriever, don’t you?” Ed replied, “Yes, I do. And it’s a real problem. I keep throwing the Labradors out of the house and he keeps bringing them back in.”

And right then, the thought went floating across my mind: I would love to live with that sense of humor every day. And that is exactly what happened.

Ed saw the world through different eyes. I would jot down the funny things he said on scraps of paper, cocktail napkins and post-it notes and eventually gathered it into a book. A friend once told me that the best place in the world to be was standing next to Ed at a party, where he would just do a running commentary on what was happening around him.

Ed made me laugh about the trials and tribulations of corporate work:

> *Manager at work:* The key to my success is that I know how to get good people to work under me.
>
> *Ed:* You’re lucky your manager doesn’t feel that way.

He made me laugh about my continual struggle with weight, and that was no easy thing:

Carrie: Your sister and her family are all so slender. I wish I had skinny genes.

Ed: You do. You just can't get into them anymore.

And this:

Carrie, doing taxes: I don't believe how much money I've spent on clothes.

Ed: Oh, it's not so bad.

Carrie, brightening: No? You don't think so?

Ed: Not after you spread it across all the sizes.

He was bemused about my self-improvement practices:

Ed: The problem inherent in all self-help books is that you are being helped by someone who doesn't know what to do.

And he definitely laughed at my spiritual adventures:

Ed: What's that book about?

Carrie: Spiritual growth.

Ed: I had that once, but I had it cut off.

But he always laughed at himself, too:

Carrie: You're doing very well in your workouts.

Ed: Yes, but it's like remodeling a house that has termites.

When we first lived together, I opened the refrigerator and saw a screwdriver sitting on the shelf. And that's pretty much the way it was with Ed. His mind was somewhere else. He couldn't find things. Well, of course, he couldn't. Who would think to look in the refrigerator for a screwdriver? So he had to buy another and another. We must have had three of everything, all tucked away in different unlikely places.

I got to live with that sense of humor and that absent-minded chaos for 46 years, something for which I am, and will always be, deeply grateful. Not only that, but Ed gave the best hugs ever.

On December 5, 2019, Ed kissed me and said he loved me, as he had done every day for all those years. Then he went outside to shovel a little snow off the driveway before going to his doctor's appointment. I went upstairs to work on a book I was writing, a precursor to this book, in which I was asking many of the questions that this book attempts to answer.

Time passed as I focused on my writing. The next thing I heard was a loud banging on the door. It was a neighbor in our town in rural Pennsylvania; she and a friend had found Ed lying in the snow as they went for a walk. As I went outside, they were applying CPR with no response. The ambulance arrived and took Ed to the hospital, where they further tried to revive him.

But the minute I saw him lying there in the snow, I knew he was gone. I remember saying, "Oh, Ed," as one might say "What have you done now?" Later, I saw on the death certificate that he had died instantly from a heart attack.

Finally, at the hospital, I was able to sit with him alone, to hold his hand for the last time, to cry, actually to wail. He had died suddenly, without a chance for good-byes, but we were in a very good place with each other; I didn't have any regrets that we hadn't told each other how much we cared. I just wanted him back. I didn't want to leave that hospital room, knowing I would never again see his dear, deeply-familiar and well-loved body.

As I sat there holding his hand, I suddenly felt his spirit lift up. It rose very, very high, very fast. Ed was an abstract mathematician and philosopher at heart; most often people had no idea what he was talking about when he was serious, so he related through that razor wit. When I felt him lift up, I sensed that he had gone to a place one might call Source, a place of numbers and symbols, the place where the universe was created. I felt that he was at peace and in a place where all his questions were answered completely, and he was understood at last.

If you would like to know a bit more about Ed, use the QR code below to see his memorial movie and to buy his book, *Edisms Revealed*, my compilation of his witty observations over the years.

By early February 2020, a little over two months after Ed died, I had packed up, cleared the house in Pennsylvania and moved back to Southern California to be near family.

In retrospect, two months seems amazingly fast to pack up and move, but I felt driven to get it done and get myself back home. In the following March, as airplane flights were canceled and we all went into lockdown from the Covid-19 pandemic, I understood why I had felt it was so urgent to move right away. If I hadn't acted that quickly, I would have been alone in rural Pennsylvania, locked down in a big house in a long, cold winter, in a town where I was still just getting to know people.

As I dealt with the grief and the wrenching transition from a loving life partnership to being a 74-year-old woman suddenly on my own, I began to understand myself as beginning the conscious process of creating a new life.

I gave my days over to grief when it came to call, often unexpectedly. And on the good days, I began to create my new life. I lost over 50 pounds—something else I felt absolutely driven to do. I also had a great desire to meditate and did so, for hours a day. I felt I was a chrysalis, dissolving the life I had known without any idea of what I would be when I chewed my way out of the cocoon and shook out my wings to dry.

I want to share with you the insights, practices, tools and techniques that truly worked for me in creating a new life. I want you to know that creating a new life is possible, even if you are older than you wish you were, even if you don't know how to be on your own, even if you think you have made mistakes in the past that have put you in a difficult position. No matter what, it is possible not only to build a new life, but to create one with deep meaning and a kernel of joy at its heart.

As for your spiritual beliefs or lack thereof, I would ask only that you open your mind and dip in a curious toe. Many of the things I am going to share with you would be called spiritual. Some are also part of a more secular mindfulness practice. Some fall into the realm of the mystic or psychic. All of them are part of Ataquay, a word I learned from the Wanataquay language. (I will tell you about Wanataquay later in this book.)

Ataquay (AH'-tuh-kway) is that place of magic and mystery, where our ordinary ideas of time, space and causality are challenged and we find that intuition is our most reliable guide. In Ataquay, we must trust what we feel in our center, see in our mind's eye, hear as a voice within and most of all, what we simply know as truth, whether or not it makes sense in our ordinary way of being.

Ataquay is the place I have been actively exploring for over 25 years and which I am presenting to you in this book. We all visit Ataquay from time to time, because it is part of human nature to live partly in our earthbound existence and partly in Ataquay. When we tell someone about our adventures in Ataquay, we often find ourselves saying: "I know it sounds weird, and it's hard to believe, but let me tell you what happened..." But in fact, the only weird thing about Ataquay is not that we go there—we all do—but that it operates under different rules.

I invite you to explore Ataquay with me as a Sojourner, one who comes here for a time, who journeys into Ataquay for the beauty, wonder and deep insight of the experience, but who can then return to concrete, practical every-day physical life when she chooses. I am not asking you to believe anything other than your own, individual experience.

And when you do return to that ordinary, so-called reality, I know you will be enriched and healed, expanded and, yes, even transformed.

Welcome, Sojourner, to Ataquay. Let us venture in together.

2 My Journey

There was nothing in my childhood to indicate that I would venture into Ataquay and spend so many years exploring there. I wasn't a fey child who had premonitions or saw dead people. I didn't even have an imaginary playmate.

I wasn't religious either. I sometimes went to church with a girlfriend's family so I could sing in the choir, but that was about the sum of my religious upbringing. I lived in an ordinary, rational world, a Baby Boomer who grew up in a San Francisco suburb, studied literature in college, built a career in the then-new field of computers and married when I was 28. And so it was, until I was 50 and Ataquay began to open to me consciously.

There were a few precursors to my experiences in Ataquay. First, I was curious about intuition. In my work with computers, I had found that when I followed my intuition instead of just analysis, I had better results. This was especially true in project planning, where I would use reason and experience to estimate how long it would take for my team to develop a computer system, then go back and increase estimates here and there based solely on intuition. And that intuition is what saved me from overrunning the budget, over and over.

I was also a singer. The first time I performed on a stage with bright lights, where I couldn't see the facial expressions of the audience at all, and where I couldn't hear them over the music, I was amazed that I knew exactly how they felt about my performance. I could feel their emotional response, from neutral and withdrawn as I first walked out, then to relaxing and warming up, and finally, when I hit the emotional core of my show, like a beautiful, powerful wave of love that flowed from them across the stage lights to me.

I found that when this deep emotional connection was made, I sometimes entered a different state, a place where the audience went away and time stood still, where I had chills and was centered completely in the moment and the song. There is also a Wanataquay word for this state: Lhamata. I will explain this word more thoroughly later.

Then there was also my experience as a songwriter. Some mornings, when I was in the shower, getting ready for work, I could feel a song coming, a piece of melody, a few words. I would jump out of the shower, grab my robe and run to my tape recorder to capture the gift of that song, because otherwise, it could fade away like a dream. I would then work further on the song during my commute on the Los Angeles freeways. Yes, I later polished the songs using my thinking brain and a rhyming dictionary, but the very best of my songs came to me first as a burst of inspiration.

If you would like to hear my music, use the QR code below to go to carriehart.com/music.

And so, on my fiftieth birthday, I was right on the edge between two worlds. On the one hand, I was completely non-religious; in fact, I had actually been considering joining an international organization of atheists. On the other hand, I was deeply curious about my personal experiences that couldn't be explained by pure reason.

On that birthday, one friend gave me Julia Cameron's book, *The Artist's Way,* along with a journal of blank pages. Another friend gave me a Deepak Chopra book, *Creating Affluence.* Both of these were new adventures for me.

I enjoyed the Chopra book and also began a practice recommended in *The Artist's Way,* of doing three pages of daily stream-of-consciousness journaling called the Daily Pages. And I loved doing it.

I think these two books, plus the daily journaling practice, helped soften me up for what happened next. I also think it's so interesting how people around us seem to give and tell us things at just the right time, almost as if angels whispered in their ears.

Here's how I finally, consciously, entered Ataquay.

One day, Ed and I were sitting out by the pool and he suggested going to the bookstore. "I don't really want to," I said. And then I thought, what am I saying? I love bookstores! So I went.

When we pulled into the parking lot of the store, I said, "You go ahead. I'll wait for you in the car." And then I thought, what am I doing? Of course I want to go in! So I did.

Once in, I went straight for the aisle I always avoided, the one marked Religion and Spirituality. I reached for a book called *You Are Psychic!* by Pete A. Sanders. You need to know here that I had never, not even during the 60's in San Francisco, had the least interest in the paranormal. But I started reading it and was so instantly engrossed that I sat down in the aisle and kept reading.

Eventually Ed came by and was ready to check out. So I stood up and put the book back on the shelf. Then I thought, what am I doing? I really want to read the rest of that book! So I slipped it under some of Ed's books as we checked out—because it was so embarrassing! Once home, I read the whole thing right away.

There are two important things about this experience. First, this embarrassing book launched me into over 25 years of spiritual exploration. I read the book, did the exercises and a whole world of experience opened up. Yes, as it turned out, we are all psychic! Which simply means, of course, that we all enter Ataquay from time to time—and we are all capable of learning to enter at will.

Second, I have come to realize that this is a fairly common pattern for me—when I am called to do something from a deep knowing inside, I often initially refuse the call; I fight against that magnetic pull.

I've since learned that this is not just my pattern. It is, in fact, an ancient human pattern, dubbed by Joseph Campbell, author of *The Hero with a Thousand Faces,* as a part of The Hero's Journey.

In the Hero's Journey, the Hero is leading an ordinary life when something disrupts his comfortable world. He then feels called to adventure and purpose, to something he needs to do that is new and exciting, but deeply challenging, driven perhaps by his gods or simply an inner sense of knowing.

Not surprisingly, the Hero often refuses the call at first. After all, answering a call is an enormously risky, life-altering event, one that sets you on a path beset by monsters you must face in battle.

Of course, when you finally accept the call—because you actually have no choice—it doesn't always feel as if you're entering a maze with a minotaur guarding the prize; sometimes it just feels like something oddly compelling that you must do without quite understanding why. And it always transports you out of your comfort zone and marks the beginning of a new adventure.

Quado

In his book, *You Are Psychic!,* Sanders suggests a particular exercise to promote your sense of intuitive hearing. Every morning, you get out a pen and paper, breathe down to a peaceful state, and then ask for a Word for the Day. Then you write down the very first word that pops into your mind.

Since I was already going down to the garden with my journal book every morning to write my Daily Pages (the journaling exercise from *Artist's Way*), asking for a word for the day couldn't have been simpler.

And it was just like Sanders said it would be: the word or phrase I wrote down in the morning would show up in mysterious and unexpected ways during the day. For example, I might get a phrase like "stay calm" in the morning only to find that someone really upset me later that day. Then I would remember my morning word and handle the situation better than I might have.

I remember one fun instance that happened at work. I got the word "compassion" in the morning, but I went through the entire workday without anything happening that required my compassion. At the end of the day, I walked into my boss's office for my final meeting of the day and on her desk was a stone with a word carved on it: Compassion. I guess my intuition was just showing off!

As I continued this exercise, I began to get lengthy messages in response to my morning request. Instead of just a word or two, I would get a page full of very good advice. I began to call the voices I heard in my head 'My Angels' and started asking specific questions about what I should do. I found that if I asked open-ended questions like "How shall I handle this problem?" that I would often get surprisingly deep and true answers, unlike my usual thinking patterns. I began taking the advice with excellent results.

I told a friend what was happening, and she said, "Oh, you're channeling." Channeling? What was that? So I looked it up on the internet and sure enough, that's apparently what I was doing. Of course, on the internet, channeling was described along with a lot of so-called New Age belief systems that didn't particularly interest me at the time.

But what I was doing was real. I was listening. Listening to voices of wisdom and truth that existed only when I breathed deeply and ventured into Ataquay.

And in case you're wondering, these voices were in my mind, not external voices. And yet, they had tone and personality, distinct from the sound of my own thinking.

Soon I began asking questions on behalf of my girlfriends. One day, I asked a question for a friend who had some serious legal problems. When the answer came, it was in a new voice. Rather than the high, ethereal voice of My Angels, this voice had more gravitas. And the answer had a definite resonance of deep wisdom.

The next day, when I went to the garden, that same voice responded to my inquiries. So I asked: "Who are you?" And the answer came: "I am Quado."

This was the beginning of a wonderful relationship. Every morning I would go to the garden, open my journal and begin writing as the words flowed into my mind. We would always begin like this:

"Quado, are you there?"

"Yes, Carrie. I am here. I will always be here."

"What message do you have for me today, Quado?"

And then would pour forth the most marvelous messages, one each day. They were always positive and loving. I began sharing them on the internet and Quado gradually gained a following. At this time, I avoided reading spiritual works or channelings by other people; I wanted to make sure I was getting just what was flowing to me without any mental filter or interjection.

Quado was my introduction to the concepts of spirituality applied to real life. Every morning, I sat on a particular garden bench for my Quado messages, a curved stone bench with azalea bushes wrapping behind it. I recall that the azaleas bloomed in November, when white blossoms surrounded me as I scribbled away, opening a pathway to a new kind of knowledge, a way I had never viewed life before.

By the way, I mentioned earlier that I began by getting messages for myself and then for girlfriends. It was quite a while before I told Ed about Quado. I had to feel secure in what I was receiving before subjecting myself to his humorous observations.

One day, after I had finally shared what I was up to, we had this exchange:

> *Ed:* "I spied on you while you were getting your message from Quado."
>
> *Carrie:* "Really?"
>
> *Ed:* "Yes, I just wanted to see you with your alien space helmet on."

Actually, I needn't have worried about Ed's acceptance. He loved abstract mathematics and as such, dealt in ideas that are much crazier than what I was doing, things like imaginary numbers and knot theory.

Now, fast forward to 2021. I signed up for a class with Lynne McTaggart in mastering intention. There were 800 of us, broken up randomly by computer into groups of 12. One day, one of the women in my group of 12 sent me an email: "I just realized why you look familiar to me. Your Quado messages helped me through a very difficult time in my life."

Ah, yes, of course. That's the way it works in Ataquay.

Running Wolf, Princess Featherlight and the Power Animals

I had been sharing Quado messages for a while when a regular reader wrote and asked me if I would do a spiritual healing session for her. I was in the middle of writing her an email, explaining that I didn't do that, when someone named Running Wolf appeared in mind and said, "Oh, yes, we do!"

So I wrote her that I would be happy to give it a try—she could be my first.

As with Quado, I simply allowed myself to be led into the new adventure, and then learned after the fact what I was doing. After I had worked with Running Wolf for a while, I read a book about shamanism to learn a bit more about what I was up to. Michael Harner, in his book *The Way of the Shaman*, defines a shaman this way: "A shaman is a man or woman who enters an altered state of consciousness—at will—to contact and utilize an ordinarily hidden reality in order to acquire knowledge, power, and to help other persons."

Yes, that was exactly what I was doing! Of course, now I call the 'ordinarily hidden reality' Ataquay.

I would (in my mind's eye) go into a shaman cave with the person for whom I was conducting the session and speak of what I saw and felt and experienced, under the guidance of Running Wolf. In the discussion below, I'll call her Naomi (Naomi was never the name of an actual client, but was a name that once came to me on an inner journey).

I never knew what was going to happen in the shaman cave, just as I never knew what Quado was going to say before the words spoke in my mind. This was the fun part for me, the adventure and discovery of new ideas. And what came was always deeply important and true, exactly what Naomi needed at that moment.

Sometimes Naomi would stand in the center of a healing circle made of stones. Chanters and drummers would sit around the outside of the stone circle, while Running Wolf stepped into the center with Naomi, chanted, shook his rattle and sometimes sprinkled powder over her. Sometimes energies would be released from Naomi and rise up through a hole in the roof, to float up to the light for purification. While this was going on, I would receive a message from Quado for Naomi.

Sometimes I would be guided to go across the cave to a staircase. We would walk down the staircase, past doors from many eras, some quite ornate, some plain and quite ancient. I would feel when it was right to open a particular door. Naomi and I would pass through the door and enter into her past life. This was particularly interesting for me the first time it happened, because I wasn't at all sure I believed in past lives! But what transpired behind the ancient door was always quite liberating and seemed to heal an old wound or simply put something in her life into perspective.

Sometimes I would be guided to go far back through the cave to an open area where we would work with Princess

Featherlight. Naomi would lie down on a bed of clouds and Princess Featherlight would work with her energies, aligning them and repairing any damage to the circulatory system, the organs, the bones, and sometimes downloading a blueprint of her body as it would have been had she done only healthy things all her life, a blueprint to guide the new cells as they formed.

Other times we would retrieve a Power Animal. We would go down the broad stone steps to the left which led to a dark pool of water. Naomi and I would leap into the pool and find ourselves going down the rabbit hole, twisting and turning, finally tumbling out into a landscape. It might be the African Savannah, or a jungle, or a forest, or even under water. We would move forward through the landscape waiting for a Power Animal to approach and show itself to us, signaling that it wanted to be with her.

She would reach out and pull the Power Animal close and then be returned to the shaman cave. Naomi and the Power Animal would lie next to each other on the floor of the cave and Running Wolf would dance around them, shaking his rattle and chanting, sprinkling powder. They would start spinning around and around, until they were a silver blur. Then Running Wolf would say: "You are now one." And so it was.

I explore the world of Power Animals more deeply in a later chapter of this book.

Buddha, Jesus and Reiki

In June 2002, I went to England to further my studies in Reiki, which is an energy healing modality. Our Reiki Master had gained permission for us to enter the center of Stonehenge after the park had closed to the public. It was evening and the wind was blowing darkening clouds across the sky. I was one of twenty on the damp grass, kneeling in a circle within the stone circle, there to receive my initiation as a Reiki Master. I closed my eyes, and the ceremony began.

I saw an enormous golden ball floating in the air above us, in the very center of the circle. Within it was a young and beautiful Buddha, sitting in the lotus position, one hand raised in blessing, glowing golden and showering his radiant energy down upon us all. I have since learned that this position is the Amoghasiddhi Buddha, symbolizing freedom from fear.

I then saw Jesus moving among us, in a robe of blue and white, weaving through the kneeling initiates, touching us, one by one. He approached nearer. When he touched me, when I felt his hand upon my shoulder, the most pure and intense love I have ever experienced flooded through me.

The peace and love I felt in that moment has never completely left me. For years after, I sensed Jesus standing beside me, his right hand on my left shoulder.

I found this first experience with Jesus to be very surprising. Since I was not raised in a religious household, I had never formed a Christian connection with Jesus. As with the other aspects of my spiritual journey, I had not gone seeking, but had in fact been found. A Hindu friend subsequently told me that this experience of grace, of receiving unconditional love through the touch of a master, would be called Shaktipat in that religious view.

When I later went to Hawaii for my attunement as a Karuna Reiki Master, I experienced a series of encounters with Jesus. My descriptions of these visions are in the Maui Papers, included in my book, *A Call to Greatness, the Exciting, Joyous Journey Your Soul Wants You to Take*, along with a more in-depth exploration of that journey.

I have sometimes worked with Jesus in private client sessions and also when I felt moved to hold a special event on a solstice or equinox. I think of Jesus as an amazing, almost overwhelming, energy force of love; there is always a wide opening of the heart to forgiveness and compassion when Jesus appears in a session, and tears nearly always fill my eyes.

My first experience with this energy was during that Stonehenge Reiki attunement and I have always felt that there was a connection between Reiki and the energy we call Jesus, Yeshua or Christ. And yes, even though I don't ascribe to the belief systems of organized religion, I understand why people say that their experience with Jesus changed them.

Deeper into Meditation and Sound

I had the great privilege of studying meditation with Deepak Chopra, spending a week deeply immersed in Primordial Sound meditation, silently repeating a personal mantra I was given. I also studied his advanced techniques, the use of Sutras associated with each Chakra. After Ed died and I felt compelled to meditate for hours a day, I utilized the techniques I learned from Chopra to excellent effect.

I have explained the Chopra advanced meditation method more thoroughly for you in the Toolkit for Vibrant Living at the end of this book, along with discussions of the other forms of meditation I have studied, such as chanting, walking meditation and a Zen technique for quickly quieting the mind.

In 2015, I studied Sound Healing, which added a wonderful dimension to my meditations and private healing sessions. This training enabled me to bring it all together, using voice, crystal bowls, tuning forks, rattles and drums, in individual practice and drumming circles. There have been studies showing that shaman drumming induces a meditative state in the brain and, of course, continually more studies demonstrating that meditation and mindful living promotes mental, emotional and physical health.

In my chapter on Grief later in this book, I encourage you to find a place where you can sound out your grief, to cry and wail loudly. I learned in sound healing that it is a purifying and cleansing thing to do, to express loudly and openly how you feel in sound. Our society's traditions of suppressing feelings, of being polite and quiet, do not serve our healing. Better it is that we wail out our pain; it truly helps us heal.

Purpose

When we signal a willingness to venture into Ataquay, amazing things begin to happen; things begin to flow to us unbidden. So it was when my purpose here on Earth was made clear to me in an unexpected way.

In June of 2006, I was sitting out on a chaise by the pool, relaxing on a lovely Southern California evening, when I suddenly heard a powerful voice speaking inside my head.

It wasn't my good friend Quado. This voice was even more authoritative. This was the voice of someone with something important to say, but once only, someone who wasn't going to be around for questions later.

So I said: "Who is this?"

The answer came: "I am he who is without a name."

I'm no biblical scholar, but I knew what that meant. So I said, "Hold it right there!" and ran inside to get my pen and journal. When I returned and resettled myself, I asked him if he would be kind enough to start over. And he did. (And yes, it came to me as a masculine voice.)

Below are the most important bits of what he said:

> *Carrie. You will fulfill your highest intention in the next thirty years. The highest intention, that you have been working toward for centuries, will be fulfilled.*
>
> *It will be revealed to you as you go along, but know this: your highest intention involves the lifting of many spirits, from one level to multiple levels higher.*
>
> *Your intention and purpose are so strong that you are deeply empowered toward their fulfillment. And all you need to do is respond to the next thing that flows toward you with deep integrity and great courage. You need do nothing more. For you are now fully riding the flow of your intended life, which*

> *means that it will all come to you. Yes, you will need to work hard, but it will also be pleasure.*
>
> *You are here to shine out with a brighter light and a higher frequency, enough so that you will lift millions of people to a higher level. This is your higher intention and you have all the power you require to fulfill it.*
>
> *What are you learning about yourself, Carrie? You can take the complex and make it understandable. But it is even more. Lift and shine. Lift and shine. Lift and shine.*

I believe all of us have the same purpose: to open ourselves to the love and light that we truly are and shine out as brightly as we can with all our glory and wonder. And, of course, to help others to do the same, in our own way.

With this mission and purpose, which we all share, life then becomes a journey for us to discover how best to express our own unique greatness and how to help others on their own personal journey of healing and self-expression. Or so it seems to me.

> *"Don't ask yourself what the world needs. Ask yourself what makes you come alive, and go do that, because what the world needs is people who have come alive."* Howard Thurman, author and philosopher

3 Wanataquay

On December 3, 2017, during a personal journey into Spirit, I was led through an energy portal of blue light, similar to the cover of this book. On the other side of this portal was an energy that was new to me. Its name is Wanataquay (wah-nuh-TAH'-kway).

I learned that it was once active in the Amazonian rain forest, two thousand years ago and more. In my mind's eye, I can see Wanataquay energy when it was active on an island in the Amazon region. I see it as a column of bright golden light, very active and moving, almost fiery, that runs down to the center of the earth and up into the heavens. Priestesses known as Ona (OH'-nuh) would gather in a circle to call forth Wanataquay energy, standing around it as it flows up and down in a column, perhaps 10-20 feet wide. Gradually, as the Ona encircle it, holding hands, Wanataquay begins to reach out and cover them in the powerful energy, which they then share with their community.

When the great indigenous cultures of the Americas disappeared, Wanataquay withdrew. I was asked to bring Wanataquay back through the portal into ordinary reality. Wanataquay is a heuristic energy and it was apparently time for it to return, so that it might learn how things are now and determine the best way to effectively accomplish its goal of bringing forth what is noble and best in human nature.

I worked with Wanataquay for a time, on my own and in sessions with several other healers, experimenting with the energy as a healing force. It learned what it needed from us and then I felt it go out into the world, seeking to know more.

Now, Wanataquay has returned to me, apparently having learned what it sought to know. I am still very much a student of Wanataquay and am just beginning to learn what this powerful energy has to offer us.

An important gift I have received from Wanataquay so far has been to learn some words in the Wanataquay language. There are four words in particular that I wish to present to you here, and which I will use throughout this book.

These words have been such a gift, because I have struggled to find a way to express certain spiritual concepts.

Most of the words in our spiritual vocabulary are so burdened with belief systems, old and new, that it becomes nearly impossible to describe a pure, personal experience without calling forth images and echoes that do not adequately reflect the clean perfection of what we actually see, feel, hear and know.

And so now I have some new words, Wanataquay words, clean and clear, free of the associations and references that lie so heavily upon the words in our own language.

To hear the pronunciation of the words of Wanataquay, use the QR Code below.

Ataquay (AH'-tuh-kway')

As presented already, Ataquay is the place of expanded consciousness, that energetic field beyond time and space we access through intuition. Some scientists have given this field the name Non-Local Consciousness. Some people refer to it as non-ordinary reality. Some call it another dimension.

I am so delighted to have a word to convey the territory I love to explore, that land of mystery that breaks all the rules we are trained to follow, the place of miracles and healing, the place where all the good stuff happens and in which the unexpected is to be fully expected: Ataquay!

Aiyama (eye-YAH'-muh)

Aiyama is your eternal, non-physical self, who resides fully and completely in Ataquay, who sees all and knows all, across time and space. The concept of Aiyama exists in many belief systems, where it may be known variously as soul, higher self, spirit, true self, or the witness. If Ataquay were the night sky, your Aiyama would be one of the stars in that sky.

Before you were born into this finite life on earth, you existed as Aiyama. You still exist as Aiyama, even if you are not consciously aware of that aspect of yourself. You will always exist as Aiyama.

As Aiyama, you chose to have an earth experience via a physical body. Someday, this life experience on earth will be over and your physical body will die and decay. Your Aiyama, however, will continue to exist and may choose to have more experiences on earth—or perhaps elsewhere.

Lhamata (lah-MAH'-tuh)

Lhamata is the state of altered consciousness you enter as a conscious sojourner into Ataquay.

I am not aware of a direct equivalent to Lhamata in the English language (although there is probably one in Sanskrit). The closest I can come to it is The Zone, a state of present moment awareness combined with heightened intuition and enhanced capability.

When you are transfixed by the beauty of the sunset over the ocean and feel time stand still, you are in Lhamata.

When you dig deep inside and overcome your fear and doubt to bring forth something magnificent and true—it could be anything from speaking a few true words to breaking a world record—you are in Lhamata.

When you are expressing your art and feel chills as you create something that later feels as if it came from somewhere else, you are in Lhamata.

When you ache with love so deeply that only tears can express how you feel, you are in Lhamata.

When you are filled with certainty about the direction you must take, in spite of many voices of reason and rationality to the contrary, and then dig deep for the courage to go your own way, you are in Lhamata.

When everything falls into place like magic and you manifest your seemingly impossible dreams, you are experiencing Lhamata.

Our ultimate goal as fully-realized humans during this lifetime is to experience Lhamata as much as possible while remaining aware and conscious of our physical surroundings, thus able to take the deep knowledge of Ataquay and turn it into effective action. When we are in the state of Lhamata, we know who we are now and can sense the next step to take with confidence and inner knowing; we feel connected and full of purpose.

When you are in Lhamata, there is no conflict and you are in your greatest peace as well as your greatest power.

Tatanqua (tah-TONG'-kwah)

A Tatanqua is an energetic presence of greatness and power that is also you, your vast potential and endlessly-expanding possibilities, made tangible in energetic form. She is the energy of your highest self, your Aiyama, brought down closer to earth, to work with you here. She is a powerful helper, but in her presence, you know that she is not external to you; she is you.

Perhaps the best way to explain Tatanqua, is to tell you the story of how I met my own.

I spent a few days in Sedona at the Enchantment Resort. On the second day, I had the good fortune of being upgraded to a spacious suite. As I walked in, the main room took my breath away. The slanted ceiling had tree trunks for beams and it soared up over a glass wall facing the majestic red rocks of Sedona, so close you felt you could touch them. I simply stood in silence, gazing out at this inspirational beauty.

Slowly I became aware of a presence in the room, as tall as that enormously high ceiling, also gazing at the red rock mountains.

I somehow knew this energetic presence as myself, but vastly more powerful than I have ever felt. I sensed her as the potential of my life, the greatness I can yet become, if I will allow myself to expand into her energy.

A Tatanqua is of this lifetime only. When this life is over and I return fully to Aiyama, she will do so as well, her work here complete. In the meantime, she will challenge me to courageous action, over and over, each mountain I climb a mere foothill to the next that lies ahead. She represents the very best I can be in this lifetime, full of resolve and commitment, nobility and dignity, strength and courage.

My Tatanqua has remained in my inner vision and I find that I can call her forth at will. I can breathe in her power and greatness. I can sense her presence when I am making important choices. I know that she will guide me in my decisions during the day and lead my steps on the path that now lies before me.

I am quite certain that you also have a Tatanqua, a great energetic presence full of courage and truth, power and confidence, waiting to be put to use in lifting you to the next level and thereby making this world a better place for all people.

***

I invite you to become comfortable with these Wanataquay words and to utilize them when the words of our language seem corrupted by overuse and fail to express your own pure and deeply personal experiences.

4 Mapping the Universe

For many years, although I loved experiencing the strange and unpredictable ways of Ataquay, I just couldn't quite make sense of it in a way that satisfied me. When I studied other people's belief systems, they just didn't feel right. Sometimes they seemed to be a variation on established religion rather than a pure exploration of the phenomena I was experiencing. Sometimes they focused on scientific evidence of the experiences, something I feel no need for. Sometimes they were simply too complicated.

Yet I yearned to have a structure of some sort to support what I have personally experienced. Somehow, after Ed died, I began to understand certain things that had eluded me.

Here is what I finally came up with, a way of looking at things from several different vantage points:

The Web

The Path of Destiny

The Layers of the Universe

The Game of Earth Life.

5 The Web

Walk with me in the early morning to see the intricate webs that the spiders have woven overnight. How beautiful they are! How they shimmer in the morning light, joining the trees together with gossamer threads.

Now, in your mind's eye, see an enormous web like this, stretching across the entire Universe. It is as intricate as those spider webs, but active, pulsating, and highly dynamic, like brain synapses. This is the Web of the Universe and it is constantly creating new connections.

In fact, the driving force of The Web is to connect. These connections are not good or bad, right or wrong, they simply are, and they are created constantly, continually.

Everything and anything cause The Web to create connections. Everything matters, everything counts. Every thought we have, every action we take, everything we hear, say, smell and touch, every person we meet, every place we go, everything we read or watch, causes a connection to be created in The Web of the Universe.

And in every moment of our lives, the Universe presents us with these connections, these pathways, as the options that we have in life. And like all of nature, it prefers the path of least resistance. Where one connection has been followed over and over, if we do not consciously direct otherwise, we will just slide down that thread again. And again. And again. The unconscious life, therefore, is one of repetition, of staying in a well-worn groove, so to speak, for better or for worse. Thus one person goes from one bad experience to another while another person seems to live a streak of good fortune.

But if we are aware, we can stop, look around and reach out to threads that we have never followed or that have fallen into disuse. We can also forge new connections, through our attention, action and conscious intention. We can choose to be a full participant in the creation and choosing of connections. And when we do this, life begins to open up and serve us fun, excitement and surprises!

Mahler and The Vision

One of my favorite examples of the Web of the Universe revolves around a truly great experience in my life, singing in a Mahler concert with the Los Angeles Philharmonic.

The story begins back in the late 1980's, when Ed and I were living in our Redondo Condo and he had a job with very long hours. I decided to fill my extra time by renting a piano and teaching myself to play.

One day, I picked up the phone and called McCabe's Guitar Shop in Los Angeles and asked about piano lessons. They said to come over that very night, because all the teachers were giving a showcase and I could pick out an instructor then. And of course the showcase was the very night I called—the Universe seems to work on a Just-in-Time principle and you need to act when the thought crosses your mind.

So I went. The piano teacher gave a little presentation and I thought, he's nice, maybe I'll take lessons from him. Then another teacher got up. His gig was a singing showcase that required an audition. If accepted into his showcase, I would get to be in a show. We would each perform 2 songs and then do backup singing for the others in the class. And it would be video-taped.

As he talked, my heart started beating so fast! A show! Yes, I hadn't known it, but that's what I wanted—I wanted to sing in a show!

I auditioned, got accepted and had so much fun, doing my solos as well as backup harmonies. It was so much fun, in fact, that I did it for several showcases. Then someone new, Sue Fink, took over the McCabe's Showcase. I worked with Sue for a few seasons and then we drifted out of touch.

Years passed. Somewhere around year 2000, I spent a week at a Deepak Chopra retreat, called Seduction of the Spirit. Every day, we spent more and more time in meditation. One day, Chopra led us in a meditative visualization. I don't recall exactly how he framed it—to see our purpose or something like that—but I saw a vision of myself standing on a stage in front of thousands of people, singing. I knew I was not alone on the stage, but there weren't any more details. Just the stage, the lights, the hall and the audience. Well, this was wonderful to me, since I had, at that time, a dream of being a professional singer.

More years passed. I did not become a professional singer, but the vision remained in my mind.

One day in 2010, I suddenly thought I ought to study sight-singing so that I would be able to pass an audition to join a choir. This is the way it often comes to me, just a thought that I need to do something, without fully understanding why. So I did.

As I was studying sight-singing, I remembered that, before we lost touch about twenty years before, Sue Fink had told me she was going to start a choir; that was her big dream. I looked her up on the internet and sure enough, Sue had built quite a successful choir, the Angel City Chorale. And guess what: they were holding auditions for the coming season. (Of course they were holding auditions right when I had the thought—that's how it works!)

I was so nervous, but I auditioned. My singing was good, but my sight-reading, although improved by the lessons I had just taken, was still mediocre at best. But Sue remembered me and I suspect that's how I made it into the choir.

Shortly after I joined, Sue announced that Gustavo Dudamel, who had just become the conductor of the Los Angeles Philharmonic, was doing Mahler's 8th, sometimes known as the Symphony of a Thousand, because it takes a thousand singers and musicians to perform it. Dudamel was reaching out to Los Angeles choirs and had invited the Angel City Chorale to come up with 50 participants. And since we were a group of 150, I would need to try out.

I wish I could find words to express how important this seemed to me. I can't recall ever working as hard as I did to learn the portion of Mahler's 8th we needed to learn for our tryout. And in case you don't know, Mahler is challenging! But I did it; I made the cut.

This was such a beautiful experience. We practiced, practiced and practiced. Finally we were joining the other choirs to practice more under the guidance of Grant Gershon, who leads the Master Chorale attached to the Los Angeles Philharmonic. We rehearsed in various venues of Los Angeles, including the Ahmanson and the new Disney Hall in the Music Center.

When I went to the Music Center for a rehearsal, they told us to go to a specific level in the underground parking. I circled down and down and then I saw the sign: "Parking for Musicians Only." Yes! That was me, a musician parking in the Los Angeles Music Center, ready to perform. I got out and took a picture of the sign. Heaven!

The actual performance was to be held in the Shrine Auditorium, a place I had never been to, because it was the only venue with a large enough stage for one thousand performers. Even there, they had to take out the first 5 rows of seating to fit us all in. 800 singers from various LA choirs and 200 musicians, from the Los Angeles Philharmonic and Dudamel's other orchestra, the Simón Bolívar Orchestra from Venezuela.

When I walked into the Shrine for the dress rehearsal, I was stunned. This was the venue I had seen in my vision at the Deepak Chopra retreat ten years before! I had made it to the future I had seen.

The whole concert was an utterly magnificent experience. To perform at this level, with some of the best singers and musicians in the world, was a dream come true.

I thought at the time that this fulfillment of a vision, so many years in the making, meant that I was destined for greatness in music. I thought it signaled the beginning of a new life. But after the concert, my life simply returned to what it was before.

Perhaps this event was meant to be for a different reason, one that went beyond my awareness and understanding. Just before we filed into the auditorium to begin the live performance, Grant Gershon, the chorale director, said: "Remember. This music is transcendent. It has the power to change the world." Well, perhaps it did.

Or perhaps it simply was. A magnificent experience for the pure sake of being. The culmination of a connection on the Web that took over twenty years to complete. Whatever the reason for this long connection, I believe that these primary events—meeting Sue Fink at McCabe's, the vision at the Deepak Chopra retreat, joining Sue's choir and the

Mahler concert itself—were markers on my Path of Destiny, one of the other concepts I wish to explore with you now.

6 The Path of Destiny

I believe one of the most important questions to ask is this: How much of our life is predetermined by a destiny, a purpose and a path we are here to walk? How much is chance? How much is free will? After seeking the answer to this question for nearly thirty years, I think I have finally settled upon the view I present metaphorically below.

Before you were born into this physical Earth life, your Aiyama (spirit or higher self) went out into the cosmic desert and laid out your Path of Destiny across the sands, placing magnetic stones along the way, each representing a milestone, an important event for you to experience as you walk through this physical lifetime. And then, at the moment of your birth, your Aiyama took a deep breath and blew, announcing your birth and causing the footsteps to disappear, but leaving the stones in place.

And even though those footsteps are now obscured, once in a while, when you are feeling deeply connected to the mysteries of this lifetime and ask for guidance, a golden footstep lights up before you, and shows you exactly the next step to take.

The magnetic force of the stones is powerful and if we stay awake and aware, we can catch the signals coming our way. Sometimes we stray far afield before we find our way back to the path that leads from one stone to the next. But eventually, we feel its pull. Sometimes we resist the pull of the stone, as when we resist the call on the Hero's Journey (I do this a lot!). But eventually we give in to our true knowing and head toward the stone. And if we become more aware and pay closer attention, we may find a more direct line to the next stone.

The active, busy mind is very little help in finding our true path. And the ego, led by the desire to please teachers and relatives, impress peers and achieve the aspirations of our culture, is most often what takes us far astray. That, and misbegotten romance.

And of course, your path is also a part of the Web of the Universe. Your ancestral and familial connections were already there in the Web before you were born. You were also born in a particular place at a particular time with certain unique talents. Perhaps there were other lives and lifetimes that had an imprint upon you. And when your Path of Destiny was laid down, The Web of the Universe instantly started connecting everything to those milestones. It connects and connects; that is what it does.

As you go through your life, The Web of the Universe connects all of your experiences, thoughts and emotions to those milestones wherever possible, taking every opportunity to lead you to those highly magnetized stones.

It is interesting to note that the magnetic stones on your path may not relate to an occupation or how you make money—although they might. Some of the stones on the path may be momentous and affect most of your life; some may be seemingly small events that don't seem particularly important to you at the time—or perhaps ever.

But these stones have a specific feeling. You are pulled toward them, with a strong sense of knowing that there is something you need to do, even if it doesn't make rational sense. You may find yourself getting ready for a milestone before it appears. I do that all the time, as I did with studying sight-singing.

And when you reach a milestone, there is a calm objective feeling about it, a sense of being in the right place at the right time. Even if you don't quite know why.

My Wedding Story

One of my favorite Path of Destiny stories is the story of my wedding to Ed, a wonderful story of serendipity and coincidence that occurred well before I was exploring spirituality. And it is, of course, also an example of the Web of the Universe doing its job to form the connections that lead along the Path of Destiny.

After a lifetime of shyness and yet with a deep yearning for a romantic partner, I finally met Ed. I was 28. That seems young now, but then it felt ancient and I worried that I would never find my true love partner.

Things happened very quickly for us. We fell in love, moved into a new apartment together and decided to get married. Then we had to decide what to do about a wedding.

I had never wanted a big wedding and Ed had already had one. I didn't want to go to a Justice of the Peace to get married—that just seemed so impersonal. And I certainly wasn't going be married by an Elvis impersonator in Vegas.

Neither of us attended any church, but that seemed like the right sort of place to get married. So I looked in the yellow pages for a fairly non-denominational neighborhood church and chose one in nearby Manhattan Beach. Ed and I met with the pastor, Reverend Calhoun, who welcomed us warmly, reassuring us that they were a community church with a lot of agnostic members. It somehow came up in our conversation that I was born in Seattle and Reverend Calhoun said that he was originally from Bellingham, Washington.

My father flew down for the wedding, he and his wife, Ann, making up the entire wedding party. As we were driving to the church, I mentioned to my father that the pastor was from Bellingham. My father was stunned. "Reverend Calhoun from Bellingham? How old is he?"

I said he looked to be somewhere in his 40's, and that was that—until my father spoke with Reverend Calhoun.

So here it is, the big coincidence, a masterful connection by The Web. By opening up the yellow pages in Los Angeles, California, I ended up being married by the son of the man who had married my parents, over 30 years earlier, in Bellingham, Washington.

And yes, it was a truly wonderful marriage, worthy of such an extravagant coincidence.

So how does it work?

I believe that my marriage to Ed was a big, powerfully magnetic stone on my Path of Destiny. And the Web of the Universe helped direct me to that path.

Of course, as always, my active participation was required. I was looking for a new job and chose the Pacific

Stock Exchange, where Ed happened to work, even though the reasoning in my head was not really on point. This often seems the case. I suspect that I receive the intuitive direction and then make up some rational reason to justify what needs to be done. "Oh, I'll take this job because I'll meet a rich stockbroker. And I can always transfer back to San Francisco, where I grew up." Neither of these happened, but it was what got me to act.

As for Reverend Calhoun and the amazing coincidence, I have found that when we do what we are meant to do, when we act upon the connection and head right for the stone on The Path, the Universe tells us that we are right by showering coincidences upon us.

I also think the Universe likes to show off, just for fun.

7 The Layers of the Universe

One morning, when I went down to the garden to talk to Quado, I saw a vision in my mind's eye. I saw the Universe as existing as a continuum, top to bottom, a gradient from bright gold at the top to dark grey at the bottom, and with four major layers that could be discerned.

The top layer was completely bright, golden light. It was what one might call The Great All or the Oneness. It was a place of pure love and light, where everything was all One.

Just underneath this, still very bright and golden, was a layer containing individual lights, just as bright as the Oneness above, but somehow differentiated from each other. I didn't know Wanataquay at the time, but these bright lights were what I would now call Aiyama (higher self). They were pure love and light, but each had a unique identity.

We'll come back to the third layer later. First, I want to tell you about the bottom layer. It was our physical existence on earth, a place of dense shadow. I could see people living their lives in this shadowy realm.

I saw one woman floating a little higher than some; she was in the lotus position, meditating. She was glowing golden and seemed deeply at peace. In Wanataquay terms, I would say she was in Lhamata. She had a cord that reached from the top of her head up to her Aiyama in the second layer. Love and light were pouring down into her from her Aiyama through that cord.

All of the people in the shadow realm had cords reaching up to their Aiyamas, but they had different levels of light reaching them in the bottom layer. A few were glowing steadily. Some got intermittent flashes of light: sometimes they were in the dark and sometimes they received a burst of light that filled them. Some had twisted cords that only let a little light through. And some seemed to get almost no light at all, living primarily in fear and darkness.

I believe that this darkness is the absence of light, not a force in its own right. And those who are without the light may do harmful, hurtful things, out of ignorance and fear, out of the absence of love and light.

Between the Aiyamas in the second layer and the shadow people in the fourth layer was the third layer. It was full of golden beings who had chosen to come down from the full light of Oneness in order to help the people on Earth. These helpers were of all kinds, representing the different spiritual and religious beliefs of people: gods and goddesses, angels, spiritual guides, ascended masters, faeries, power animals, and ancestors.

You can call these helpers what you will, and you can picture them however they seem to you, for they all have exactly the same purpose. They are there to help people strengthen their connection to the light, to straighten out the cord, to open the channel to the Aiyama so that love, light and wisdom pour down and the people can live lives full of love, joy, health, meaningful work and abundance.

We could describe this third layer as Ataquay, the mysterious place beyond space and time, where all the good stuff happens. When we go into a state of Lhamata, we lift up into Ataquay and find that we are surrounded by help.

Quado helped open the golden flow of energy to my Aiyama, so that I might learn how to live in peace and truth and teach those principles to others. Running Wolf, Princess Featherlight and the Power Animals are all there in Ataquay, helping my clients to open the golden cords to their individual Aiyama.

8 The Game of Earth Life

I can't leave the exploration of the structure of the universe without telling you one more point of view that was revealed to me quite recently.

I was driving back from the grocery store, when I felt it beginning, wanting to flow over and within me. It was so strong, I pulled over to the side, parked the car and just let it come. I closed my eyes and listened to my mind grow completely quiet, yet deeply energized. A major idea was upon me, filling me. And soon it would want to be expressed.

I sat in the car and simply let the energy surround and enter me wordlessly. Then, as I drove the rest of the way home, the words began to form. When I arrived home, I went straight to my computer to capture the part that I had already received, as well as open to the rush of new words.

Elizabeth Gilbert, in her book *Big Magic*, talked about a creative Idea as tangible energy that is floating around looking for someone to receive it and give it form. When it comes to you, if you refuse to write that book or song—or even procrastinate too long—the Idea moves on to someone else for expression. That's how tangible this felt.

So here's what came to me. What if I, Carrie, this apparently flesh-and-blood person here on Earth, am not quite real? What if I am a character in a game, the Game of Earth Life?

Could it be that the "real" me is playing a computer game and I, Carrie, am simply a projection from that?

Now, before you reject that idea completely, please think of what the physicists tell us. They say that we are not really solid at all, that we are really just a collection of atoms with spinning electrons. I read an explanation once that said we could think of solid, physical matter, as being like a fan. When the fan is not turned on, you can put your hand right between the blades, but when it is spinning, you cannot move through it—as if it were solid. And so we are like that—as is the chair we sit in—just energy spinning so fast and in different frequencies, that it all seems solid.

Not only that, but they say that this spinning matter is mostly space. To give an idea of the matter-to-space ratio, if the nucleus of an atom were the pitcher's mound, the electrons would be spinning at the outer edge of the baseball stadium. And all the rest is empty space.

And so, given all that, why couldn't we just be projections of energy like holographs, pawns in a game played at a higher level? And for all I know, the entity that is playing me could be sitting on the holodeck in a starship, just like Star Trek. In fact, let's call her Captain Hart.

As I sat in my car, a lot of ideas came floating in about how this might work. Things that actually make some sense, in a strange sort of way. Here's the detail that came to me.

Game Setup

The character Carrie was set up before play began. Captain Hart defined me to the computer before she hit GO and started my Earth Life. She made choices like these:

Female

Heterosexual

Human

Gemini

Born in Seattle, Washington

Music lover with nice singing voice

Highly intuitive

Not very athletic.

Captain Hart also created a Game Plan with major milestones at approximate ages, like marriage, children, careers, accomplishments and death. This Game Plan is my purpose, or destiny, my path. Of course, these milestones are not made clear to the characters—after all, this is a game! The milestones and opportunities exert an unexplained magnetic pull, but one that can be resisted through personal will or ignored if the character is swept away or distracted by the many allurements of physical Earth life.

Captain Hart also chose Helpers to assist me, selecting from a pantheon of gods, angels, emissaries and others. For me, Carrie, she selected a spiritual guide named Quado, a shaman named Running Wolf, power animals and a few visions and voices.

Captain Hart chose a level of difficulty, indicating the type and force of challenges I, Carrie, will face as I attempt to carry out my Game Plan: physical, mental and emotional challenges; devils and demons; enemies and tempters; personal weaknesses.

And the computer that runs the game? It is called Chance. Of course. Every game must have Chance at its core to make it fun.

After the game was set up, Captain Hart hit GO and play began. Now it's up to me, Carrie, using my so-called Free Will, to play out my Game Plan with Chance rolling the dice, tossing out random events for me to deal with.

And here's where the fun really begins, for neither Captain Hart nor Chance control the actions of the other people I encounter during Earth Life. Meeting them might be a part of my Game Plan, but they were created by other crew members on the starship holodeck, acting out their own Game Plans, and it's up to me, Carrie, to act in response to what happens, to foil my enemies and avoid my tempters, and possibly to call for help to those angels and gods provided to me.

At the moment Captain Hart hit GO, I, Carrie, became a live spark in the womb of another active game character, my mother. Captain Hart then had approximately 9 months in Earth Time to decide whether to abort the game. She did not and so I was born into Earth Life. At the time of my birth, any memory of being a character in a game was erased and will remain so until my game ends with my death in the Game of Earth Life.

There may be occasional leaks and bugs that break the standard Game of Earth Life rules. After all, no computer system is perfect.

One apparent leak is that I can sometimes get a glimpse of another character that Captain Hart played in a previous game. These are often referred to in Earth Life as Past Lives. I can also get an occasional glimpse of Captain Hart herself, as a feeling or a glow, a golden light in my center that feels truer than the character I am playing. In Earth Life we may call that a Soul, Higher Self or Aiyama, an eternal spirit I will return to when I die.

But the biggest leak of all is this one, the one I am experiencing right now, which lets me see myself as a character in the Game of Earth Life.

So what is the greater purpose of the Game of Earth Life?

Maybe, like most games, it is simply entertainment, a fun way for Captain Hart to pass the time. In that case, as Shakespeare's Macbeth said, Earth Life may simply be "a tale told by an idiot, full of sound and fury, signifying nothing."

Truth?

I explored this idea for a time. In fact, I began a previous version of this book based on the Game of Earth Life idea, in which Ed and I were both officers on a star ship, and we were setting up the parameters for the Earth Life Game we would play together, how we would meet at work, be married by the son of the man who married my parents and then play for another 46 Earth years.

So now, you might well ask, is this what I really believe, that we are players in a game being run on a star ship holodeck?

Well, no, I couldn't say that. In my heart, I far prefer the Web of the Universe, The Layers of the Universe and the Path of Destiny. I'd like to think there's a deep meaning to my life, some reason I am going through all the sound and fury, enduring the slings and arrows of outrageous fortune.

And so, you may be wondering why I even included the Game of Earth Life here, for your consideration. And, actually, I did go back and forth on that decision.

I finally decided to include it to demonstrate that all of our belief systems are metaphors for what we do not—and cannot—fully understand. If you take any belief system, the ones I've presented earlier as well as any other spiritual or religious view, can you prove that it is more valid than the Game of Earth Life? No, I don't believe you can.

And so, we are left with Shakespeare's Hamlet, who said it best: "There are more things in heaven and earth … than are dreamt of in your philosophy."

Yes, I believe that is true, that there is much more than we will ever understand. But it is also true that we can make the best of it, creating a life full of beauty and wonder for the time we are here. We can choose metaphors that empower our lives, actively selecting those that shine with love, rather than darken with fear, those that inspire and expand us rather than those that dampen and limit us.

Yes, let us do that. Let us create a beautiful life, right now, a life that dips deeply into the wonder that is Ataquay.

9 Grief

I wrote this book to share with you what I have learned about creating a wonderful life, no matter what. But if you are creating a new life for the same reason I am, then we must first deal with grief.

Grief is the worst, because there's nothing for it, no way to fix it or hurry it. We just have to go through it in our own way and in our own time. Actually, not in our own time—in grief's own time. Because grief will pour out its tears whenever it chooses, surprising us over and over. Just when we think we are handling things well, grief opens our hearts anew to let us know that the well of tears is not yet dry.

A friend of mine, who lost her child, said "grief is not linear." And this is so true. It is not a steady climb out of the depths. The oddest thing, an object, a photo, a sound or smell, will suddenly strike you and bring you to your knees.

I don't expect life to ever be the same as it was before. But I believe we can learn to create a life full of beauty, wonder and yes, even joy, even without the one we have lost, even on our own. Life is resilient. Spring always comes again and if we allow it, we can open our hearts to the daffodil pushing through the earth, striving to reach the sun and live. We can step outside, breathe the air and feel the sun on our shoulders. We can choose life.

Your grief is your own personal journey. I can only share what helped me, in hopes it may be of some assistance to you.

Don't be Afraid of Grief and Don't Try to Fight It

Grief can have surprising depths. At some point in the months after Ed died, I went for a walk, alone. I sat down to rest for a moment and was suddenly overcome by a wave of grief that felt endlessly deep. In that moment, which I can still picture so vividly, I fully understood why women pulled out their hair, wailed and threw themselves on the burning pyre. That was what I wanted as well.

And yet, the tears eventually stopped. Grief somehow completed its cycle, at least for that moment. When we give in to grief, we may be afraid we will go endlessly deep, but we don't; eventually this episode ends and we stop crying. For now.

This level of grief is elemental, as old as the human race and quite rightly the stuff of stories thousands of years old. It has a kind of purity, when we allow ourselves to feel it fully. The catharsis of grief fully expressed is purging and purifying and, in its own strange way, rather beautiful. After all, it is only your capacity for deep love that can bring you to inexpressible grief. And that capacity is a deeply human gift.

I found that it helped to be noisy. Yes, noisy, really noisy. Yelling, wailing, sobbing without self-consciousness. I would go for a drive, park somewhere away from everyone and let it all out. Sitting there in my car, I had my own version of shaking my fists at the sky, falling to my knees, wailing and pounding the earth. I could cry loudly until I could cry no more.

After I was done grieving out loud, I would feel relief in my body. And when it built up again, I would go for another drive.

Releasing Blame

Somehow, we have to find a way to release guilt, shame, self-recrimination and blame. Not everything was the way we wanted it to be. We did things we regret and left many things undone and unsaid, that we wish were otherwise. The loved one we grieve was not perfect either, nor were the various family members and caregivers involved. There is ample blame to go around.

We need to find a way out of these feelings. They are corrosive and will harm us. They lead into depression and despair and will keep us from healing. They will also keep us from the healing catharsis of pure elemental grief.

The way out is to learn to pay attention to our thoughts. Notice the thought that crosses your mind. If you are new to this, it may help to write down the primary, repetitive thoughts, so that you are clear about what you are thinking.

After you learn to pay attention to your thinking, the next step is to change it. Do not accept that your thinking is truth, for it is not necessarily true at all. It is a point of view you have been trained to. We are used to looking at life in a certain way, perhaps with shame and self-blame, for example, and this point of view is expressed in thoughts that say, over and over: How could I have done that? Why didn't I do this or that?

Of course, I catch myself with thoughts just like that. When I do, I say to myself: It doesn't really matter now, does it? I did the best I could; so did he. We both did the best we could, being who we were at the time.

Your goal is to come to a place of acceptance of what was done and left undone, because it is absolutely true: it doesn't really matter now. No amount of shame or blame is going to change the fact that your loved one is no longer here in physical form.

> *"To realize that you are not your thoughts is when you begin to awaken spiritually."* Eckhart Tolle, author of *Power of Now*

Combat depression

When we lose someone we were living with, someone who was a part of our daily life, we not only have grief to deal with, we have a whole life to reconfigure, a new role to occupy. It is quite wrenching to go from being half of a couple to being on your own. It takes time to figure out who we are in this new role. And there will be times, of course, when we lose the battle with our thoughts and begin to slide into depression.

I read once that depression is the result of thinking that nothing will change, that the current state of anxiety, fear and confusion will never go away. But, like so many of our thoughts, that is simply not true. Everything changes. Nothing stays the same forever, good or bad.

When I feel myself starting to slide, I notice my thoughts and try my best to turn them around. Sometimes I'll notice my mind telling me: "Oh no, I'm getting so depressed. I can hardly move or even breathe. Here it comes."

When I notice this, I take several deep breaths—breathing deeply always helps, doesn't it? Then I remember that my thoughts are not truth; they are something I have trained myself to accept, a point of view I can change.

I do my best to consciously say an opposing thought. "Actually, I am all right. In this moment, right now, I am OK. I am strong and I can handle my life. I own my life and my thoughts. I am all right."

Amazingly, when I bring myself into the present moment, I find that I actually am all right, right now, in this now moment. I remember that my obsessive thoughts are focused in the past, where blame, shame and guilt reside, or in the future, where fear and doubt hold sway. When I come fully into now, in this moment, somehow everything is all right.

And while I am in the present moment, sometimes I sit down with pen and paper and fill a page with gratitude. I know that sounds a little corny, a little over-simple. But amazingly, it works. Once I start, it's easy to keep going, and I find there are plenty of things to say, like this:

- I am grateful for my cat, Abby.
- I am grateful for the tree outside the window and the bird I hear singing right now.
- I am grateful for my sister, who just called me to make sure I was OK.
- I am grateful for all the years I had with Ed and how much we loved each other; I know how lucky I am to have had that.
- I am grateful for the beautiful music I am listening to.
- I am grateful that I am healing.

And then, focused in the present moment and with a heart full of gratitude, I pull back the drapes and let the sun in, go for a walk, move. In other words, I choose life.

> *"If you are depressed, you live in the past. If you are anxious, you live in the future. If you are happy, you live in the present."* Lao Tzu, Ancient Chinese Philosopher

Living Alone

My first reaction to living alone was not only feeling adrift and unanchored, but also being afraid. When I had last lived alone (46 years before!), I was sometimes lonely, but never afraid. I think that part of the recent fear was that I had become accustomed to feeling a man's presence and it felt so odd and unsettling to have that missing.

But the bigger part of the fear came from being older and alone. We have all heard the stories of older women who fell down and broke a hip, couldn't get up or reach the phone and weren't discovered for days. That's a pretty scary thought.

This feeling of fear does gradually pass and after a while you grow to enjoy having your own space, where things actually stay where you put them. In the meantime, you can always get a wristwatch that detects a fall, or one of those devices that you wear around your neck. I didn't do either of these, but they're certainly worth consideration if it helps.

Here's what I did that I highly recommend. This was my sister's suggestion, and it has been wonderful. Every morning, I play a game on my smartphone called *Words with Friends 2.* It is a free telephone app, in which two people take turns to play Scrabble.

I am an early riser, so I take my turn first thing with my cup of coffee. Then my sister takes her turn later in the day, when it works for her. Not only do I feel a daily connection with someone who cares about me, but I also feel safer. Because she knows that if I don't play my game, and I don't text her why I'm not playing, that there may be something wrong and that she needs to call me—and if she can't reach me, to call someone local to check on me.

We now play four games simultaneously and I look forward to my coffee and game time every day. It's fun, it makes me feel connected and safe and it gives me a little daily brain exercise to boot.

Talk to your loved one

"Death is a stripping away of all that is not you."
Eckhart Tolle

I have found that the energy of people who have died can be quite tangible, especially in the weeks and months right after death. I find it perfectly normal to hold conversations with them. Really. And I'd like to tell you about my experience with my father and with Ed.

I loved my father and took it hard when he died. One night, not long after he died, my father came to me in a dream. At this time, I was getting up every morning before dawn, wrapping myself in a blanket and going down to the garden to channel messages from Quado.

So when my father showed up in my dream, I grabbed my pen, journal and blanket and headed out to the garden. I received a beautiful message from him, all about how much he loved me, my sister and his wife, Ann. He wanted to be certain that we knew that.

I received several more messages from him, but interestingly, with every message, he was growing younger and his focus was less on us and his life on earth and more on the next adventure he was about to have. In the last message I had from him, over twenty years ago, he was a young man, full of vibrant energy, ready to find out what was to happen next and turned outward to the Universe.

Some months after Ed died, I realized that he and my father were together. I found I could ask the two of them to just let all their love flow down in one big, beautiful energetic hug.

While I was meditating one morning, I felt a most beautiful stream of energy pouring down upon me. First, it was Ed's love, pure and strong. Then he mixed in his pride and admiration for how well I was doing. "I'm so proud of you!" he said. And then my father joined in and poured down his love and pride as well.

Then they both poured out gratitude for all the gifts I had brought to their lives here on earth. And I just lay on my bed and opened wide to receive it all, with tears and gratitude of my own.

I feel that they want me to be strong for the years I have left to live. They want me to choose life and to live it in joy.

Whatever it is that lies ahead, I know I will be able to handle it and they will be there to cheer me on.

As you read this book, I hope that you find comfort in the ideas I present and also learn, if you don't know already, how to reach the world of mystery and love that is there for you. I know you can. You don't have to wait until you die to be with those you love; they are around you right now, pouring out their love upon you. Not as they were in life, no, that is true. But still, it is something. It helps.

Denial

After about a year of grieving, I met a woman whose husband had died 5 years before. I asked her if I was through the worst, if it was going to get better now. She told me that her second year was actually harder than the first, because she was in so much shock and denial the first year; it was in the second year that she finally came to terms with it.

I think my dreams tell the same story.

In the first year after Ed died, I didn't dream of him at all, even though I was dreaming quite vividly. But in the second year, I had two dreams that told me what my subconscious was up to: it was moving out of denial and into processing that this was, in fact, a new life.

The first of these dreams was pretty straight-forward. I was looking for Ed and couldn't find him. I ran around asking people: "Have you seen Ed? I can't find him!"

Finally one of the people I asked this of gave me an answer: "Oh, he died. Didn't you know?"

And I woke up with a start and a pain in my heart.

The second one was even more wrenching. I was in the kitchen with Ed and it was completely normal, just talking and fixing dinner. And then I suddenly got excited as I realized what was happening and said: "Wait a minute! I thought you were dead. But you're not! You didn't die! You're alive!"

I was so gloriously happy that Ed was alive and in the kitchen with me. It had all been a mistake! My life was normal again.

But then came the next thought. Oh no, what if I'm dreaming? What if this is just a dream and I'm going to wake up and find out that it's true, that you died!

And then, of course, I woke up. And well, you know the rest.

And you, too, will process your loss in your own way and in your own time. Perhaps, like me, your dreams will tell you what is happening at a deeper level.

My Theory of Grief

Here's my theory of deep grief. I think it's a wound in your energetic field. And that feeling you have that part of you is missing? I think you feel that because it's true.

Our entire physical presence, after all, is really just a bundle of energy, consisting of atoms with spinning electrons. And when you live with someone, sleep with someone, touch, hug and kiss for year after year, it makes sense that your energy would get mixed up, that in your body, you would be carrying energy you picked up from him and vice versa.

So I believe that when your husband dies and leaves his physical form, the energy that belonged to him gets pulled out of the physical realm. And that includes the energy that is actually residing within your physical body. I think it can be a violent and sudden physical separation that leaves you wounded and bleeding. And grief is the time of healing that wound, a healing that is highly personal and takes as long as it takes.

I want to tell you what happened to me, that led me to my theory of grief.

About two years after Ed died, I suddenly felt something shift. In some ways, I hadn't fully realized the depth of my pain until, one day, that pain actually lifted. The sudden cessation of that psychic, energetic pain made it clear what agony I had been in for all that time.

And now, I have found that this impression of being energetically healed was true. I feel that I am through the worst of it. Yes, I still miss Ed and think of him many times a day, often with sadness and sometimes with tears, but also frequently with sweet memories and gratitude.

But the primary shift is that I feel as if my energy field has somehow knitted and become whole again. I feel complete. And as I say, I think this is, in fact, a physical reality. I think it will happen to you, as well, in your own time, especially if you look for healing within Ataquay.

No, of course, we won't ever "get over it." But there is an enormous difference between being sad and being in agony.

And after my energy wound healed, I had my first peaceful dream about Ed. We were sitting under a tree and talking about life. There was no anguish during the dream or when I woke up. Does that signal a new stage of acceptance and healing? Yes, I believe it does.

Community

I didn't feel a need for a large community when Ed was here. Most often, just being with him was enough. After he died, when the initial support and attention was over and people went back to their lives, I realized that I needed to actively build a wider circle of friends. After all, I could no longer just turn to the person next to me and ask if he wanted to go out to dinner or a movie tonight.

Now I had to arrange something, to invite someone to go out with me. And obviously, it would be easier to ask a friend who was on her own. So, if you don't have a ready supply of such friends, you need to get out and find them. Yes, you do. Because sitting home alone and feeling sorry for yourself is not a kind, loving and healthy thing to do to yourself.

And what does this mean? It means, for some of us, that we have to get over our shyness, insecurity and questionable confidence and just do it. And what do we do? Everything we can think of. Join groups. Volunteer for a committee. Take classes. Try a lot of new things. Take a deep breath and walk into functions alone, then look around and see other people who could use some company and just walk up and say hello.

Is this comfortable? No. Is it scary? Yes, especially at first. It is possible, even for someone shy? Yes. Does it get easier? Oh, yes, much easier. The more we do it, the easier it gets. Is it fun? After a while, believe it or not, sometimes it actually is.

Can you do it? Yes.

And after a while, when you feel you have almost too many things on your plate, you cut back on the activities and people that you didn't really connect with that deeply and focus on what works for you. And one day you look around and voilà, you have new friends and activities for a new life.

Two True Thoughts

Sometimes I find that the only way to approach the deepest, truest thing is to express two thoughts, both true, and yet opposite, opposing, contradictory. And so I offer these two thoughts as the signposts of grief, between which there may be some sense of ultimate truth.

Here is one thought:

> How can this be? How can it be that I will never again hear your voice, feel your touch, and experience the utterly unique wit and wisdom that kept me laughing and confounded for 46 years? It is such a loss, an irretrievable loss, and such a waste! It's hard to believe that life simply goes on anyway, without you here. How can that be? How can it be right that you are gone?

And here is another thought, equally true:

> Nothing is lost. I feel your presence; I know you are here. All of your love still surrounds me and it sustains me and allows me to move forward, to

> choose life, to be and even to expand into all that I am, even though, my love, you are no longer here beside me. Even though I can no longer hug you or hold your hand, I can still close my eyes, take a deep breath and feel your love all around me.

I know and I experience both of these as truth, right now, and all the time.

And so, we keep going. We choose life.

Or, as Ed always said: When the going gets tough, just put one foot on the top of the other.

10 Embracing the Mystery

The Toolkit for Vibrant Living, which follows, contains all the wonderful tools and techniques that have helped me. But it is so important that I not give you the impression that following these practices, as wonderful as they are, gives you control, that these are magic formulas that guarantee that your life will be just the way you want it.

It is all so much more complex than that. In fact, I feel absolutely confident in telling you that we truly have no idea how things work. Sometimes the Universe responds to our intentions—and I very much enjoy sharing examples of this with you. But sometimes, no matter how hard we try and how much we want something, it is simply not given to us. And so now, I would like to share a personal example of this.

But this is not a tale of disappointment. It is a complex tale that has many opportunities to look at the Universe in different ways, and to draw your own conclusions—or to join me in shaking your head in wonder at the mystery of it all.

My House

Ed and I had been living in a condominium in Redondo Beach for about twenty years, when we happened one day to go for a Sunday drive. We drove up into Palos Verdes, which is a beautiful community on a hill above the Pacific Ocean, full of eucalyptus trees and custom homes with red tile roofs, of that style that Californians call Spanish. And of course the street names are all Spanish, with Via this and Paseo that.

We spotted an open house and decided to go in. Oh, my. It was love at first sight.

I remember thinking that this was exactly the kind of house that doctors lived in when I was growing up—you know, in that time of the 50's when doctors were on the top of the social and financial ladder. And this actually turned out to be true; we later learned that the house was originally built for Dr. and Mrs. Tuttle in 1950.

It was big, with what the realtor called 'generous' rooms. As a big, tall guy, the size felt just right size to Ed. And it had a swimming pool, something I had always yearned for. And even a bit of an ocean view. Yes, here it was, the house of our dreams.

True, it was a bit dated, but I loved that about it. The bathrooms had colorful tile that looked as if it might be original. The kitchen had been updated, but I guessed that had occurred sometime in the 70's, probably when the family room was added. But it was all fine with me, exactly as it was.

And best of all, the house spoke to me. I knew it wanted me to live there. It literally felt enchanted to me—and this was before I was at all interested in anything remotely resembling enchantment. I just knew that I was meant to live there.

I was making a good living as a Vice President and CIO (Chief Information Officer), which, together with a dip in the real estate market around then, put the house within reach. I don't recall what Ed was doing then—I think he was consulting in the computer field—but I know he was gainfully employed at something. In short, we actually qualified for a big mortgage on that big, beautiful home. And that alone was quite a miracle.

The house did not disappoint. It was a joy to live there. And of course, it was here that I began my spiritual journey, going down to the garden to talk to Quado every morning before dawn, sitting on the bench surrounded by white azaleas.

The Corporate Gig Ends

After a time, Ed had some personal struggles and was unable to work. But I had moved on to an even more lucrative position, again as a corporate Vice President. Ed and I had a pretty expensive lifestyle, with that big house and a sailboat as well, but my executive salary covered it all.

Then, the company I worked for was acquired by a company near Philadelphia. At some point, I was given a choice: either move to Pennsylvania or accept a severance package of a year's salary.

Well, I had this dream that I could make a great living doing my spiritual work, if only I had the time. So here was that opportunity to see if I could make a go of it. Also, I absolutely did not want to leave my wonderful home in California and move to Pennsylvania. So I accepted the severance package.

I did develop a business and make some money, but the income certainly didn't approach the level of my corporate executive income, which had included bonuses as well as a great salary. I did computer consulting to augment the business income, but basically it wasn't working financially and Ed was still unable to work. Debts kept creeping up along with the property taxes and I felt enormous financial pressure. And if you've ever lived in an older house, you know that there is a lot of expensive, on-going maintenance as well as sky-high utility bills.

However, I still believed in the dream, the dream that I could support us as we wanted to live, staying in our beautiful house, doing work I loved and that was truly helping others. I worked very, very hard and I also called upon all of my energetic tools, things I've included in the Toolkit for Vibrant Living at the end of this book, plus many more. I must have tried every technique for abundance manifestation that anyone has ever devised!

I also asked to see a vision of my future, to see what important milestone was coming next on my Path of Destiny. What I saw was my house in Palos Verdes, beautifully maintained. I was standing just inside the entrance foyer, greeting people. I couldn't tell what the occasion was for the gathering, but I imagined all sorts of wonderful things and took it as a sign that I would find the financial wherewithal to continue to live in my wonderful home.

The Dream Ends

Years passed and when I asked, I still saw the same vision. We continued as we were, sometimes almost catching up financially, but overall falling behind with the pressure mounting.

One day, I was sitting outside by the pool, as usual doing energy work to manifest my dream, when it came to me like a flash, like a bolt of lightning. It was such a strong and sudden knowing that I said it out loud: "What in the world am I doing?"

I suddenly realized that it didn't matter how much I wanted what I wanted. I knew that this wasn't going to work. I ran in and told Ed: We have to sell the house and the boat. Now.

I reached out to people, looking for advice on where to move and what to do there. I was offered a job by a client, helping to bring about a more spiritually-oriented culture in her company, and I accepted it. Interestingly enough, it was in Pennsylvania, the state I could have moved to as an executive, with that great salary, some years before.

In any event, we fixed up the Palos Verdes house, staged it for sale and put it on the market. The realtor set up a table in the entrance for the open house. A few people were arriving as I walked into the foyer—and I was stunned. There it was—my vision of greeting people in the foyer. As it had in the vision, the house looked beautiful, with the sun pouring in through the stained glass window and open door. And people were coming in, picking up the sales brochure.

Imagine that. For several years, I had taken that vision as a sign that I would be able to find a way to stay in my beloved house. And all along, it was a vision of its sale.

Pennsylvania and Back

The job that took me to Pennsylvania didn't work out, but my time in rural Pennsylvania gave me many gifts. I made some wonderful friends and ended up working in the world of politics, which was new and very interesting, something I am continuing to do.

When Ed died, two years after our move to Pennsylvania, I returned to Southern California to be near family. My daughter had heard of an apartment that was available. It turned out to be in Palos Verdes, just down the hill from our old home, on the very same street. And that is where I live now.

The money we made on the sale of the big house in Palos Verdes, together with some gains from the house we had in Pennsylvania, has enabled me to do my spiritual work with financial freedom.

I heard a speaker recently who said that sometimes you just have to let go of what you love dearly to let your life open up and evolve. Or, to paraphrase the Rolling Stones, you can't always get what you want, but sometimes you get what you need.

What Does It Mean?

So we end here with the questions posed at the beginning of this book. How much of our lives is free will, how much is chance, and how much is destiny? How much do our intentions influence our path? Or is it all a cosmic Game of Earth Life?

Or how about this? Let's just embrace the mystery. Let's explore, experiment and expand. And yes, let's allow ourselves to love deeply when we can and then let go when we must.

TOOLKIT

FOR

VIBRANT LIVING

11 How to use the Toolkit

In the Toolkit for Vibrant Living, I present the best of the tools and techniques that I have tried in my many years of spiritual and mindful exploration. Some of these I have channeled from my helpers in Ataquay. Many of them I have learned from books I have read and conferences and classes I have attended over the years, often modifying them later, as I worked with them.

For some of you, who have been on a spiritual path for a time, many of these tools will be very familiar and you may wish to lightly skim until you come to something new or rediscovered. I have chosen to include everything that I personally found useful, since some of you are new to this adventure and others may have taken different paths than mine.

If you are new to spiritual practices, I invite you to proceed sequentially, exploring and experimenting as you go. Please disregard what doesn't feel right to you and modify the rest to suit you personally. And then let them evolve into your own set of tools.

12 Healing the Past

This section provides some concepts and helpful techniques for correcting how our past has settled into our body and mind.

Owning Your Body Weight

I've always thought it interesting that we humans so often focus on trying to control things around us and outside of us, like other people's behavior, while failing to control what we actually can: our own thoughts, actions and reactions. For example, I have complete responsibility over what I put in my mouth, and yet I have spent most of my life struggling with my weight.

About six months after Ed died, I suddenly knew that the time had come to end the struggle and lose some weight I had been fighting for years, weight I had lost and regained many times over. This came as an absolute knowing. I went on a strict diet and didn't cheat even a spoonful until I had lost 50 pounds. I have managed to keep most of the weight off, but it continues to be a challenge.

I know how difficult this topic is. But if we are serious about creating a new life, this needs to be a part of it. How can it not? For so many years, all plans had to start with "First, I'll lose 20 pounds. Then I'll do it." I'm running out of years in which to do that—I need to live now!

One of the things that I found very helpful was the affirmation for "Fat" in Louise Hay's book, *Heal Your Body.* I memorized it and said it over and over to myself during those months of dieting—and I still do, and not only in situations that involve eating. Here it is:

> *"I am protected by Divine Love. I am always safe and secure. I am willing to grow up and take responsibility for my life. I forgive others and I now create my own life the way I want it. I am safe."*

The main thing I want to say is this: It's worth doing, for your mental and physical health. And yes, you can do it. No matter how old you are (I was 74, after all). No matter how many times you've tried and failed. This can be the time you succeed. The past does not have to be a repeating pattern.

You can change. This time, you can do it.

For myself, I need to continually adjust my attitude, so that I don't feel sorry for myself and fall into victim thinking. Perhaps it's harder for me than for some others and perhaps not. But it doesn't really matter, does it? We all have our challenges and this is mine.

Is it worth making this a high-priority focus? Yes, I do believe it is.

Owning Your Thoughts and Emotions

It may sound odd, but our thoughts do not always speak the truth. They are a reflection of what we were taught to think, by our parents, teachers, peers, coworkers and the overall culture in which we live.

> *"What a liberation to realize that the 'voice in my head' is not who I am. Who am I then? The one who sees that."* Eckhart Tolle, author of *Power of Now*

In his wonderful book, *The Four Agreements*, Don Miguel Ruiz talks about how we were domesticated, taught what to think and how to behave through reward and punishment. Our minds remember this and repeat it back to us, over and over, so that we no longer need to be rewarded or punished; we have taken over that job ourselves.

I read once that baby elephants are trained to stay in one place with a chain attached to a stake pounded into the ground. The adult elephant could obviously pull up this stake at any time, but does not. He is trained. He is now the one who keeps himself imprisoned. We do this with our minds, that voice we listen to that tells us what to do and what not to do, that tells us whether we're good enough to receive the bounty of the world.

In order to choose happiness now, we need to pay attention to our thoughts and turn them around, replacing fear, anxiety, doubt, criticism and judgment with something kinder and gentler. We can learn to be a good friend to ourselves as well as others.

Begin by noticing your thoughts. Write down your main thoughts, if that helps you. Then, begin to police your thoughts, replacing the negative and judgmental thoughts with positive affirmations. When you catch yourself thinking negatively, stop and immediately turn it around.

For example, you hear your thoughts saying: "I can't believe I did that. How stupid of me!" You can notice the thought and turn it around: "I always try my best. Sometimes I learn by making mistakes. It's all right." And of course, you can extend this same thought to others who make mistakes.

And it is always good to say Louise Hay's favorite affirmation: "I love and approve of myself."

Does all this sound corny and over-simplified? Yes, I get that. But it does work.

If you find yourself being overly critical of others, listen carefully to your thoughts. You are undoubtedly treating yourself to the same level of criticism and judgment, and probably far worse. Begin there, with gentle loving thoughts of how amazing you truly are.

NLP

NLP, or Neuro Linguistic Programming, is a technique to help people change how they respond to the world by changing aspects of their internal unconscious view. Many life coaches and business coaches use it to empower clients to change unwanted behavior and achieve their goals. It is also used in sales and negotiation training to help people establish rapport and reach mutually-satisfactory solutions.

NLP is meant to be used by a trained practitioner, but you can also study it for your own benefit. I would like to share now my experience with one technique that I found to be very simple and very effective. If you decide to try this and it doesn't work for you, please don't write NLP off—just realize that your internal triggers may differ greatly from my own—what I've shared below is my personal experience, to give you a little understanding of the process, not a comprehensive presentation of NLP.

Here's my personal experience in using a technique with the totally non-poetic name of Cross Matching Submodalities. NLP seems to favor mind-numbing names to describe mind-opening techniques!

My background story: Every morning I would tell myself to do my little 20-minute set of physical exercises, but most days I simply wouldn't. I would find other things to do and the day would just go off on its own way. I felt there was some kind of resistance happening, but had no idea what or why. (By the way, one thing I loved about this NLP technique, was that I didn't need to know why the issue existed in order to correct it.)

Here's what I did. First, I was to think of a moment in my life in which I was just completely happy and at one with the world, a time when life was glorious. For me, I pulled up a particular memory.

When we were living in Pennsylvania, I would get up first and normally be in the kitchen when Ed arose. He would walk into the kitchen and I would wish him good morning and then throw my arms straight up in the air, my signal that I wanted a hug. He would smile and move in to give me a big hug and a kiss. And in that moment of being hugged, I couldn't have asked for anything more from life. So that was the moment I chose as my happy memory.

The NLP technique is to take your wonderful, totally positive memory and ask quite a few questions about it, taking note of the answers. Among the questions were these, with my answers in parentheses afterwards:

- Is the picture still or a movie? (movie)
- Is it in color or black and white? (color)
- Is it near or far away? (very near, a few inches in front of my nose)
- Are you experiencing it from within your body or looking at yourself from afar? (within my body)
- What size is the picture? (life size)
- Is it framed or panoramic (panoramic—it even wraps around me)
- Is it bright or dim? (quite bright)
- Are the colors intense? (yes, very)
- What do you hear, if anything? (a sigh of contentment)
- What do you feel, if anything? (warmth and gentle pressure on the front of my body)

Next I was to erase that picture and then picture the thing I was resisting and apparently didn't like, but that I wished to like and include in my life because it was good for me. In my case, this was doing my set of morning exercises.

So, I pulled up a picture of me doing my exercises. When I looked at this mental picture, I was amazed to see that the characteristics were quite different from my happy picture. Here it is:

- Is the picture still or a movie? (movie)
- Is it in color or black and white? (color)
- Is it near or far away? (far away, beyond arms length)
- Are you experiencing it from within your body or looking at yourself from afar? (from afar)
- What size is the picture? (little)
- Is it framed or panoramic (framed by fuzzy edges)
- Is it bright or dim? (dim)
- Are the colors intense? (no, not at all)
- What do you hear, if anything? (a grunt of effort)
- What do you feel, if anything? (not sure, perhaps a little muscle pain)

So now, here's how I applied the technique. I looked at the exercise picture in my mind and changed the characteristics to match those of the positive hug picture. In other words, in my mind, I did this to the exercise picture:

- I brought the movie picture closer and stepped inside my body, so I was experiencing it, not keeping it at arm's length
- Now it was quite large and panoramic
- I made it brighter and increased the intensity of the color
- I imagined a sigh of contentment to replace the grunt
- I felt warmth and love on my body.

And an utterly amazing thing happened: I jumped up and did my exercise routine! And the next morning, all I had to do was call up that big, colorful picture again and once more, and I felt fully motivated to do my exercises.

The example above is how it worked for me. For you, you might have much more emphasis on how it felt or how it sounded. But I did want to give you an idea of both the power and the simplicity of the techniques, in case it's something you wish to pursue further.

NLP Circle of Excellence

Here's an example of something you can use right now, my variation on an NLP technique called Circle of Excellence:

1. Stand up and visualize a big circle on the floor in front of you.

2. Fill the circle with as much joy and love as you can, pouring it right out from your heart, remembering the beautiful moments of your life or creating them from your hopes and dreams. Connect with the emotion deeply.
3. Fill the circle with confidence, clarity and courage, the kind of confidence and courage you admire in others, the kind you have shown in strong moments. Re-experience those moments.
4. Fill the circle with appreciation and admiration for all that you are, your best qualities, the parts of yourself that you love.
5. Fill the circle with your full potential, everything you want to be, everything that you are when you rise to your greatness.
6. Now, step into the circle and breathe it all in, let it soak into you, be it completely. Feel the emotional intensity of the most wondrous you.
7. When you're saturated with happiness, step out.
8. Every morning, just before you get out of bed, see the circle on the floor, right next to the bed.
9. Now step right into the circle and breathe in all the wonder that you are.
10. Be happy!

"There is no way to happiness. Happiness is the way." Thich Nhat Hanh, author of *The Art of Living*

Energy Healing Systems

"It's supposed to be a professional secret, but I'll tell you anyway. We doctors do nothing. We only help and encourage the doctor within." Albert Schweitzer, M.D.

There are many energy healing systems that work to support and awaken our body's natural ability to heal, for example: acupuncture, acupressure, Qigong, homeopathy, essential oils, flower essences, Emotional Freedom Technique (aka EFT or Tapping) and Reiki.

It is well worth your while to explore the different techniques. Many people turn to these alternative therapies only when traditional Western medicine fails them, but if you experiment and explore, you may find some therapies that work well for you as a first response.

Below I explore some systems that have been particularly helpful to me as well as some overall considerations in delving into energy healing. If you are interested in this topic, I highly recommend a book that provides a wonderful starting point to your own exploration: *Radical Healing* by Rudolph Ballentine, M.D.

Doubt and Belief

Western society has done an excellent job of sowing doubt about our abilities to handle our own health ourselves. Western medicine teaches us that our health is to be managed from the outside in, by taking pills and submitting to treatments, like surgery, and that there are very specific experts, like doctors and surgeons, that we can trust to tell us what to do. Our society has granted these experts great authority over us, as evidenced by the fact that they are among the few people we still address by a title.

It takes courage to trust yourself, to believe that you are capable of healing your own body. For this reason, I encourage you to explore some healing modalities when the stakes are fairly low, so that you have the knowledge of what might work for you when you are in a critical state. You may find, as I have, that some healing modalities are better suited for your body, mind and spirit than others.

Just like Western medicine, not all treatments work equally well on all people. And not all practitioners are a great match for you either. If you want to own your own healing, you will need to spend the time and energy to find out how your body responds to various treatments.

If you doubt that you are capable of healing yourself, please take a moment to think about placebos. In order to get a new drug approved for use, the pharmaceutical developer must demonstrate that the drug is actually effective, that it does a better job of curing the disease than nothing at all. This is done by trials in which some people receive the drug being tested and some receive a placebo, a pill that looks the same but does not contain the active ingredient being tested.

What is interesting about this, is that there are always a certain number of people in these drug trials who are "cured" by the placebo. The drug companies ask us to believe these people are a bit crazy. One must ask, what is happening here? There are people who receive what they believe is a miracle drug and who are indeed cured from what they thought was incurable, but in actuality they received nothing. Nothing but belief.

During the drug trials, the caregivers are also prevented from knowing which pills contain the drug and which are placebos. Why? Because the belief of the caregiver can also influence the results.

So belief matters, yet it can be difficult to believe what everyone in your society and family has told you is untrue. I would encourage you, therefore, to learn what the Energy of Belief is for you and utilize it, even if you still have some doubts. You can train your mind and body to believe, until the day that you truly do. As they say, fake it 'til you make it.

The Energy of Belief

Your first task is to feel the difference between the energy of Belief and the energy of Doubt.

Think of something you truly believe you can do. It doesn't need to be difficult or unique; driving a car, using a cell phone or baking a pie would be fine, but something you're particularly proud of would be even better.

Now, picture yourself doing this activity and being proud of your ability, while you say, "I believe, in fact I *know*, that I can do this." Notice how you feel. You should feel expansive and open, chin up and chest lifted. Notice how bright the light is.

Next, think of something you are not at all sure you can do, perhaps something you would love to do but have struggled to learn. For many people, this could be related to accounting or math, or possibly learning a language, playing a musical instrument or public speaking.

Now, picture yourself doing this activity and feeling your doubt in your ability, while you say, "I don't know that I can do this." Notice how you feel. You probably feel smaller and contracted. Your chest and arms probably cave in; you slump and you look down. Notice how dim the light is, how shadowy.

This helps make it clear why your belief is important. I know that when I did this, I could feel how my Belief Energy would send a very clear signal out to the Universe, whereas my Doubt Energy just sent a fuzzy, confused cloud of energy out. The Web of the Universe truly wants to connect and the clearer the signal, the better the chances that a true connection can be made.

Now, your job is to bottle the Energy of Belief.

- Take 3 deep breaths while standing with confidence, arms up, chin and chest high.
- On the first breath, fill yourself with love for yourself. Say it out loud: " I love myself exactly as I am!"
- On the second breath, fill yourself with gratitude for being you. Say it out loud: "I love being me! I'm so lucky to be me."
- On the third breath, see yourself doing the activity that gave you the strongest belief energy. "Yes, I can do it! In fact, I am really, really good at this!"
- See all the energy, light and bright, that is within you and around you.
- In your mind's eye, hold out a bottle and watch this energy pour into it.

- Put in the stopper. Set the bottle of Belief on a shelf in your mind.

Now, whenever you want to do energy work, take down that bottle, open the stopper and take a deep breath. Ah, yes, you can do it! And say to yourself: "I believe, in fact I *know*, that I can do this, that I will do this, that I am doing it right now."

You can do this when you practice any Energy Healing systems and when you practice Intentions as outlined later in the Building a Vibrant Future section.

Homeopathy

Homeopathy is a deep area of study, and not my area of expertise. But it is useful to know about it and perhaps dip your toe in a bit.

Homeopathy was discovered in 1796 by Samuel Hahnemann, a German doctor. It works on the basic principle of 'like cures like':

homeo = similar

pathos = suffering.

Thus you take a homeopathic version of poison ivy (rhus toxicodendron) to cure ailments that have symptoms similar to poison ivy.

Homeopathic medicines are diluted and shaken ("potentized") beyond the ability to detect the substance; the more diluted the substance, the more powerful its effect. Because of this extreme dilution, there are those who say they can't possibly have an effect; but in fact, they do.

Another important concept in homeopathy is: less is more. When it begins to have an effect and you start to get better, it is important to stop taking the homeopathic treatment. Otherwise, it may have the opposite effect.

I like to think of homeopathic treatments as containing information and energy that tells your body how to heal itself. And once your body get the idea and takes over, you need to stop telling it what to do. No one likes a nag!

There is an excellent presentation on homeopathy in the book I mentioned earlier, *Radical Healing by* Rudolph Ballentine, M. D.

Some homeopathic treatments are beginning to be mainstream and available in most drugstores. Arnica is one such; it helps sprains, strains and bruises heal in a fraction of the time.

EFT (Emotional Freedom Technique), also known as Tapping

The purpose of EFT is to reduce physical or emotional stress by tapping on the ends of meridian points. The easiest way to learn it is to watch this video of Gary Craig, the founder of Tapping, and then use my steps below as a reminder of his instructions:

Some people have found EFT to be very effective for eliminating phobias and pain. Some practitioners seem to think you can accomplish almost anything with its help, like wealth attainment. That hasn't been my experience (and believe me, I tried!), but I do think it's worthwhile to experiment with it and see how it works for you. It's so simple and I think it's useful to have in your toolkit.

EFT Process:

First, identify something you wish to make better, physical or emotional, e.g., stiff neck, depression, fear of flying, any repetitive issue or worry. Give it a number of discomfort, 1-10, where 10 is high discomfort.

Now go through the tapping sequence, as follows:

1. Tap the side of your hand (karate chop) while saying: "Even though I have this stiff neck (or fear of flying, depression…), I deeply and completely love and accept myself." **Do this 3 times.**

2. Tap the top of your head 5-7 times, saying “this stiff neck”
3. Tap at inside the eyebrow 5-7 times, saying “this stiff neck”
4. Tap at the side of the eye 5-7 times, saying “this stiff neck”
5. Tap under the eye on bone 5-7 times, saying “this stiff neck”
6. Tap under the nose 5-7 times, saying “this stiff neck”
7. Tap between lower lip and chin 5-7 times, saying “this stiff neck”
8. Tap just below your collar bone points, down an inch, out to side an inch, 5-7 times, saying “this stiff neck”
9. Tap under your armpit (on bra line) 5-7 times, saying “this stiff neck”

Assess the discomfort now. Is the number lower? Did something else come up? Do it again and again, watching the discomfort number decrease.

If you like, end with a tapping cycle of positive affirmation. (I am free of…)

Reiki Healing

I think that Reiki should just be something in everyone’s personal first aid kit, a standard part of everyone’s lives. After all, we are built to heal ourselves and if something can help trigger the self-healing mechanism, we should welcome it as perfectly natural and normal.

Although I now think of Reiki as simply natural, when I consider it from the perspective of what I believed before I began my spiritual explorations, it is actually rather astounding.

Here's a brief history. Reiki, which is Japanese for Universal (Rei) Energy (Ki), was "discovered" by a Dr. Usui, who was born in Japan in 1865. They say he went on a 21-day retreat up Mount Kurama, and when he returned he had the gift of Reiki Energy in his hands. He used Reiki in his practice and passed it on to several other people during his life. One of those Reiki Masters was Mrs. Takata, who brought it to the West.

Reiki is passed from Master to student through what is called an attunement, a ceremony in which the Reiki energy is passed from one person to another using various symbols. Over the years, different Reiki Masters have taken Reiki in various directions, using it differently, teaching it in various ways and expanding and developing new directions and techniques for its use.

But the basics are the same: Reiki is a specific healing energy which activates the self-healing mechanisms of people. The ability to use Reiki for healing is intentionally passed from one person to another. Before Covid-19, Reiki attunements were normally done only in person; now, people have accepted that remote attunements can be just as effective.

When Reiki is applied in healing, the energy passes through the hands of the healer to the body receiving it; it does not drain any energy from the healer.

I have received Reiki Master level attunements in three schools of Reiki: Usui, Karuna and Holy Fire. Here are some of my observations about Reiki:

- When receiving Reiki, people seem to sense it differently. Some have told me it feels like heat. Some say they can feel and even see energy flowing.
- When I am giving Reiki, my hands feel energized. When the flow is very strong, my hands feel as if they are stuck to the person receiving the energy; when their body has received enough, my hands feel released.
- Reiki does no harm and has no side effects.
- You do not have to believe anything specific for it to work. The person receiving it does not even have to believe it will work. It just does.
- It works beautifully in relaxing muscles and relieving pinched and stressed parts of the body. A kink in the neck, for example, gives way to Reiki nicely and predictably.

- I find that Reiki works very well in treating injuries that have just occurred, but that for old injuries, where your body has been compensating and correcting for some time, it is much less effective and its effects may be temporary. I suspect it simply takes much more time and patience, over multiple treatments, to correct older ailments.
- Some people seem very receptive; I can just feel their bodies suck in the energy through my hands. Other people feel a bit resistant and take longer to get Reiki energy flowing.

Here are some of my favorite personal examples where I used Reiki.

When we were cruising in the British Virgin Islands, my grandson wiped out surfing and got cut and scraped on some rocks. When he returned to the boat, after everyone finished fussing over him, I asked him if we could do an experiment. I gave him Reiki on half of his body, on the injuries that were the worst. The other half we left alone. There was no immediate effect. But the next day, the difference was apparent. The cuts that had not received Reiki were bruised and puffy. The cuts that had received Reiki still showed as cuts in the skin that had not yet healed, but there was no bruising or puffiness.

In another instance, I was working as a consultant training people on a computer software application. One student was quite late; she said she had been rear-ended driving back from lunch. As she talked, I could feel my hands energizing, just itching to be used. I asked her to sit down and I put my hands on her shoulders, letting Reiki flow down her body. I drew a picture of a Reiki symbol that felt right for her and asked her to look at it. I actually taught the class that way, with my hands on her shoulders as she gazed at the Reiki symbol. Her body was soaking in the energy and suddenly, we heard her back crack, just like a chiropractor giving an adjustment.

In yet another instance, a friend called because her boyfriend had just injured his knee badly while playing basketball. I focused and sent remote Reiki to his knee. The next day it was completely fine, as if nothing had happened.

As I said, on the one hand, it is just perfectly natural and normal self-healing. On the other hand, it's a little miracle you can very easily learn to use.

13 Centering into the Present

This section focuses on ideas and techniques to bring you into a calm, centered place, right now, no matter what.

Love

Love is the grease that makes the wheels of the Universe turn. It is the emotion that lifts and elevates all activity to the highest level. It is the great motivator, the force that moves mountains. It is what makes life worth living and helps us bear what we must.

It is also the power that drives our ability to create the life we want. When we fill our hearts with love for what we want, the Universe shares that love and works with us to create it.

Love is the ultimate positive thought and emotion. And Love's friends are kindness, sympathy, empathy, care, support, forgiveness, turning the other cheek, giving the benefit of the doubt, assuming the best, joyful anticipation, beauty, acceptance, tolerance, grace, order, openness, curiosity, expansiveness, lifting, fluidity, laughter, inclusion, clarity, insight, gratitude, humility, self-love, self-acceptance, warmth, connection, community, confidence, courage.

Fear is the ultimate negative thought and emotion. And Fear's companions are doubt, shyness, self-consciousness, hatred, intolerance, criticism, judgment, prejudice, willful ignorance, giving no quarter, assuming the worst, playing devil's advocate, chaos, dread, anxiety, stress, small-mindedness, closed-mindedness, rigidity, anger, exclusion, denial, resistance, blame, revenge, defensiveness, arrogance, coldness, resentment, withdrawal, apathy, jealousy.

Take three deep breaths and then read the last two paragraphs again. As you read about the friends of Love, pay attention to how you feel, how your heart opens and expands, how good you feel. As you read about the companions of Fear, feel how you close in and get smaller, how bad you feel.

That energy we feel, of Love or of Fear, is very real, and it forms the foundation for the life we are creating in every moment, whether we want to or not. We are creating our lives from our thoughts, emotions and actions. And we get to choose whether we wish to create a great, expanding life of Love or a small, shrinking life of Fear.

The Circle of Love and Life

Picture the concentric circles that result if you toss a stone into a still pond. There is a little circle in the middle that creates circles that reach out and out.

The circle in the middle is you, your truth, who you truly are. Getting to know who you truly are is the foundation for all love and for life creation. How can we survive the loss of loved ones, if we don't understand ourselves as strong, individual beings with the right to exist, alone and with others? How can we love ourselves if we don't know ourselves? Deep within you is a core of peace and love. It is a place you can go to whenever you like, a place of love and safety, no matter what.

The next circle out is love for yourself, a deep love of who you are in your core and approval and acceptance of who you are in the world, just as you are, in your perfect state of imperfection. What we wish to achieve is to hold these two thoughts at one and the same time:

> I love and approve of myself exactly as I am right now.
>
> I am evolving into the next truly wonderful way to be.

The next circle out is creative self-expression. Every day, every moment, we are telling The Web who we are and the life we wish to create. We do it through how we dress, the home we live in, the food we cook and eat, the way we move and carry ourselves, the beauty and art we appreciate and create. When we take loving care to express who we are in every way, the Universe pays attention and brings us more of what we express. And of course, if I am not showing who I truly am, how can those who are looking for someone just like me, find me?

The next circle out is love of others, loving relationships, community. How I treat myself and others is a mirror reflecting back to me. Again, The Web makes connections for us based on what we express through our thoughts and actions. If I want criticism, anger and defensiveness, then being that will return that to me. If I want love, kindness and consideration, then the more of that I give, the more of that will flow to me.

The last circle is our place in society, the jobs we hold, the money we earn and receive, the status we achieve, our celebrity, our marital status, our outer beauty. So often, people's wishes focus directly here, but all of this is ephemeral. It all shifts and changes throughout our lives, affected greatly by circumstances outside our control. But it is also affected strongly by our center core and the concentric circles that led out to it. And so, we must begin at the center of the circle and move outward.

> *"When we seek money, or a good relationship, or a great job, what we are really seeking is happiness. The mistake we make is not going for happiness first."*
> Deepak Chopra, author of *Creating Affluence*

Your Morning Practice

I wish for you that you may love yourself enough to establish a morning practice, a defined set of activities you perform every morning, without fail, ideally when you first get up. Yes, you may need to get up earlier than you do now in order to fit it into your schedule. You may need to ask someone else to help you, to take over certain duties so that you can do this. If you live in a busy household, you may need to get up a half-hour before everyone else in order to get the peace and space you need. But it is worth it. It will utterly, completely, change your life and move you from Fear to Love.

The remainder of this section will describe some elements that you could incorporate into your Morning Practice. It is up to you to try these things and decide what you like and what seems to work for you. Note also that it is a dynamic process, in which you continually reassess what works in a particular phase of life, letting your morning practice evolve as you do.

Here are the constants that will help you create and maintain a morning practice:

- Do your practice at approximately the same time of day, every day. Just before dawn is excellent for me; find out what works for you.

- Do your practice in the same location, indoors or outdoors. It helps to have some beauty in that place, perhaps sitting by a window with a tree outside, perhaps fresh flowers on the table.
- Create a bit of ritual. I like to light candles. I also use the same soothing music every day. I will often start and end by speaking aloud the same words. For example, I might start with "I ask for clarity and loving guidance" and end with "I give thanks."
- Do the same things in the same order until you consciously decide to do something else.
- Always begin with deep breathing to reach down into peace.
- No rushing, pushing or desperation; calmness is your goal. If time is limited, then set a timer with a low, soothing sound and do your practice until the timer sounds. Your cellphone is perfect for this.
- Do not skip days. Limit the time when you must, but show up every day.

The reason for all of this is the same: to trigger your mind and body to enter a peaceful, receptive state. If you follow these guidelines, you will find yourself automatically becoming calmer when you sit down in your peaceful place and begin your practice every day.

Deep Breathing

If you're not sure about the effect of deep breathing upon the body, put your hands on the shoulders of someone who is tense and stressed. Ask them to take three deep belly breaths, as described below. Your hands will feel their shoulder muscles relax in response to the breath.

Nothing could be simpler than deep breathing. Do this while you are learning how:

- Put your one hand on your chest and one at your waist
- Breathe in through your nose, counting silently to 4
- In your mind's eye, watch the breath as it enters your body
- Bring the breath all the way down to your belly, so that the hand on your chest does not move and the one at your waist expands
- When the belly is full, then fill up the chest, if you like
- Hold your breath for another count of 2 to 4, whatever feels right
- Exhale through your mouth, making an audible sound, for a count of 4 to 6, whatever feels right
- Watch the breath as it leaves your body.

Breathing Down

If three deep breaths are not enough to clear your mind and relax your body, if you are very tense and seem unable to reach a peaceful state, try breathing while silently counting down from ten to one, as follows:

As you breathe in, count silently to yourself: ten, ten, ten

As you breathe out, count again to yourself: ten, ten, ten

As you breathe in, count silently to yourself: nine, nine, nine

As you breathe out, count again to yourself: nine, nine, nine

As you breathe in, count silently to yourself: eight, eight, eight

As you breathe out, count again to yourself: eight, eight, eight

Continue as above, until you reach one. By one, you should be much more relaxed.

If not, start over again at ten.

Present Moment Awareness

Here is one very simple technique that is especially effective when you wish to bring yourself out of disturbing thoughts and emotions and into now:

- Breathe deeply and notice how the breath travels through your body
- Look around and notice what is actually around you, all the details you normally don't even see
- Close your eyes and notice what you feel, the chair under your bottom and against your back, how your heart is beating, cool metal against your skin, fabric texture under your hand
- Smell the air, inhaling deeply
- Take a drink of cool water and feel it all the way down into your body; notice what your empty mouth tastes like
- Listen to all the noises you rarely even hear, the fan in the room, the wind in the trees, the birds singing to greet the dawn.

Gratitude

When I am going through a difficult period, I will often add gratitude statements to my morning practice, especially if I feel I am on the verge of slipping into depression. Just take a piece of paper and fill it with simple statements of gratitude, like this: "I am grateful that my friend, Mary, called me yesterday to talk."

There is always something to be grateful for, if you give yourself a moment to reflect. And you will always, always, feel much better as a result.

Meditation

> *"To know yourself as the Being underneath the thinker, the stillness underneath the mental noise, the love and joy underneath the pain, is freedom, salvation, enlightenment."* Eckhart Tolle, author of *The Power of Now*

I highly recommend a daily formal practice of meditation. Do it every day and you will find that it has cumulative effects. It is excellent training for becoming aware of your thoughts and calming them down, creating open space between your thoughts and building a peaceful center inside.

Even a meditation session you think of as difficult or unsuccessful, where your mind is overly active, still has its effect. Just do it!

"God is in the gap between thoughts." Deepak Chopra, MD, author, mind-body-spirit leader

I think of meditation as a way of reaching peace and also a way of receiving from the Universe. If you are unsure of exactly what you want, or if you are going through a major life transition and have no idea what will happen when you emerge from the chrysalis of change, meditation will help you calm down and receive guidance.

I sometimes ask for guidance just before I meditate. I ask that guidance may flow to me and that I may walk my path easily. I ask that my desires may be congruent with the path I am here to walk.

Meditation Basics

There are many forms of meditation, some of which I will explore later. Here are some basics to bear in mind, whatever form you decide to practice:

- Start with 3 deep breaths or with breathing while counting down, as described earlier.
- Set a soft timer to 20 or 30 minutes, or use timed background meditation music.
- Some recommend meditating twice a day; I normally meditate only once a day.
- When you are pressed for time, one 5 - 10 minute meditation is better than skipping altogether.
- Meditation is most often energizing, not sleep-inducing, so first thing in the morning is excellent as is

the end of your workday; late at night may disrupt your sleep.

- If you're a yoga practitioner, lotus position on the floor works, but for most of us, simply sitting in a comfortable chair is easier.
- Sit comfortably, feet flat on the floor, hands in your lap or on your thighs.
- Lying down is also OK, unless it makes you fall asleep.
- Eyes can be closed or simply lowered, whatever works for you.
- If you use the same location in your home every day, it helps cue your body.

It is normal and natural to have thoughts cross your mind while you meditate. When you notice them, just allow them to drift by, perhaps even as clouds floating by.

It is also normal to sometimes get lost in a train of thought. When you notice this, just gently return your focus to your mantra, breath, music or guided meditation. There is no need to criticize yourself for this; just deal with it easily and gently.

If an urgent thought comes ("Oh no, I forgot to call the babysitter!"), I just jot it down on a piece of paper and return to meditating.

Chanting

Chanting is another form of meditation. My favorite is to go to this video and sing along with the Tibetan monks:

If that link doesn't work for you, try entering "om mani padme hum" in the YouTube search.

Om mani padme hum is a traditional Sanskrit mantra; the exact meaning doesn't quite translate to English, but I understand it is basically about compassion. One thing I love about the chant is how it carries with it the thousands of years it has been in practice by people striving raise themselves up to a higher level.

You may notice that what the monks are singing is a little different than how you think you should pronounce "om mani padme hum." They are using the Tibetan pronunciation, which is "om manee peh-may hung." Just close your eyes and sing along. You may notice that after you complete your chanting, if you sit in silence, the chant will echo in your mind. If you are having trouble quieting your thoughts, try chanting out loud for 5 minutes and then doing a silent meditation; the echo of the chanting may replace your repetitious thoughts.

Mantra Breathing Meditation

The use of a mantra helps you focus. There are many Sanskrit mantras in wide use. Here is a very simple mantra anyone can use, that I got from Deepak Chopra's book, *The Spontaneous Fulfillment of Desire*: So Hum, meaning, in Sanskrit, I Am That.

Close your eyes. As you breathe in and out, watch your breath, entering and leaving your body.

Silently say "so" on the in-breath and "hum" on the out-breath. If you find your mind drifting, then gently return to your mantra. That's it.

If you prefer, you could watch your breath and silently say "I" on the in-breath and "Am" on the out-breath. As I said, I rather like the energy of a Sanskrit word that has been chanted for thousands of years, but it is entirely your choice.

Walking Meditation

Thich Nhat Hanh, a Vietnamese Zen Master and author, recommends a walking meditation, simple and effective. Just go for a walk alone and get into a nice walking rhythm. As you walk, bring yourself into a state of deep connection with the present moment, using nature to help you do this. Listen to the birds, look at the clouds and trees, notice each flower along the way, breathe in fresh air, say hello to the neighbor's cat. As with any form of meditation, if your mind begins to drift, just gently pull yourself back to the present moment, feel your walking stride and embrace the wonders of life that surround you.

And yes, this counts not only as meditation, but also as exercise, a wonderful two-for-one. Walking with a friend and chatting away, however, counts only as exercise.

Guided Meditation

Use the QR Code below to go to the Meditation page of CarrieHart.com, where you will find recordings of several guided meditations that were channeled from Quado.

I would recommend starting with the Self-Love Meditation. All of the Quado meditations begin with the breathing countdown described above. These guided meditations are an easy way to begin a practice of meditation, since all you need to do is listen.

Chakra Meditation

When I studied meditation with Deepak Chopra, he taught us a meditation in which you move your focus up the chakras, picture the color for each chakra, and repeat specific words, called sutras. You can just think of chakras as energy centers in your body; the locations are described below.

Chopra gave us 4 words for each chakra. Repeat each word 4 times, approximately 15 seconds apart for a half-hour meditation (7 chakras * 4 words * 15 seconds = 28 minutes). You can memorize the chakras and words below and estimate the time between words, or you can listen to my recording, which you will also find on the Meditation page of CarrieHart.com

Chakra 1: Tailbone, Color Red

Flexibility, Transformation, Coherence, Stability

Chakra 2: Reproductive Organs, Color Orange

Purity, Nourishment, Charm, Merging

Chakra 3: Solar Plexus, Color Yellow

Desire, Intention, Will, Destiny

Chakra 4: Heart, Color Green (traditional) or Pink (my personal preference)

Peace, Harmony, Laughter and Love

Chakra 5: Throat, Color Blue

Creativity, Affluence, Abundance, Discernment

Chakra 6: Third-Eye, Color Indigo (a dark blue)
Integration, Truth, Unboundedness, Knowingness
Chakra 7: Crown of Head, Color Violet or White
Infinity, Immortality, Holiness, Enlightenment

In the early stages of grief, when I had absolutely no idea what to do with my life, I found this meditation very helpful. I memorized the words and said them silently to myself, this mental activity making it easier to stay focused. I said each word 4 times, but didn't worry about how long I took between words. Sometimes I would linger on one set of words, feel them and contemplate their meaning in my life.

Doing this daily over a period of weeks (or was it months?), I felt myself clearing and cleansing and then loading myself with the kind of energy I wanted to take forward into my new life.

Look at those words again. Isn't that what we want in our lives? Isn't that what we want to load into the Web of the Universe and ask it to deliver to us?

Zen Quiet Mind Technique

This is a variation on something from Eckart Tolle, the author of *Power of Now*.

I think of this not as a daily meditation, but as an emergency tool to quickly reach at least a few moments of peace no matter where or what. It is particularly useful at 3 in the morning if your mind has fallen into an obsessive, repetitive thought loop and you just can't seem to break the pattern. Just continue to lie in bed, but do this exercise.

It can also be used before your regular meditation when you feel very scattered and deep breathing doesn't seem to be enough to settle you down. You may do it sitting or lying down, however you normally meditate.

Here's the technique:

1. Bend your dominant arm at the elbow, so that your hand is not touching anything.
2. Close your eyes and take 3 deep breaths.
3. Silently ask: How can I know that my hand exists?
4. Feel the energy leave your busy mind and flow into your hand, as its only way of answering the question.
5. Notice that your mind grows completely quiet for a blessed moment.
6. If your mind starts chattering again, just ask your question again and observe how the mind quiets as the energy flows to the hand.
7. If you like, you may lift the other hand as well and ask your question for that hand.
8. Do this as long as you like.

Channeling

I consider channeling to be a form of meditation. I suspect that it is one of those things that everyone can learn, but which comes easily and naturally to those of us with high intuitive listening skills (see my later discussion on Intuitive Senses). I would recommend that you try it, but don't push it if it isn't fun and easy. Some people channel into physical sensations or seeing visions, not into words, so don't concern yourself if this doesn't work for you.

I began by writing what I received from Quado in longhand in a journal. When I was sharing my channelings with others, I grew tired of the time it took to transcribe my channelings, so I learned to channel while typing at the keyboard, capturing it all as it came and then correcting the mistakes later with spellcheck. After that, I wanted to do readings with clients on the telephone, so I learned to speak aloud what I was receiving, as it came to me. All of the methods take some practice to master.

I also started small in what I was requesting. I began by asking for a word for the day and jotting down the very first thing that crossed my mind. Then I began to ask if there was a message for me and wrote down the full message in my journal, writing as the words came. Just open to the flow and keep writing without stopping and never, ever, edit what you receive at the time you are channeling. Your job is to quiet your own thinking and be a pure channel for receiving and recording. You can analyze it later.

Of course, like any meditation, channeling begins with breathing, breathing yourself down into a calm, receptive state.

When you are channeling aloud, you will find it helpful to have a routine, a place you go in your mind's eye that you can describe as you begin. This signals your body to go into a receptive state and hand over control.

When I began channeling Quado out loud, I would go into a cave, saying "Down, down, into the cave, down into the cave" as many times as it took to get myself into Lhamata (the zone), a buzzy feeling you will come to learn. I would then go to a deep pool of water full of answers, and there, at the edge of the pool, I would say, "Quado, are you there?" and open my dialogue.

Later, when I was doing healing sessions with Running Wolf, the cave became a shaman cave and I led my client in, saying "We are outside the shaman cave and now we go in. The stone floor is cool and smooth under your bare feet and you can see the reflection of the fire flickering on the cave walls." As I did this, I pictured the scene and felt myself lifting into Lhamata.

One of the first shaman practices I learned was a power animal retrieval, in which you go down a passageway to the

Land of the Power Animals. I did this by jumping into the very same pool of water that I knew from my previous Quado channelings, twisting and turning and then tumbling out into a landscape where a Power Animal awaits.

The shaman cave opened its secrets to me gradually. I simply went wherever I was led, speaking aloud of what I saw as it came to me, from healing circles surrounded by chanters and drummers, staircases leading up to higher levels of consciousness, staircases leading down to doorways into past lives, and various special chambers in the cave to which I was led.

But all of that is my adventure, my journey. For you, who knows? Just quiet that busy mind and allow yourself to experience the mystery that wishes to unfold to you. Allow truth, your truth, to reveal itself in your very own way.

Happiness

Our western culture teaches that we will be happier when our circumstances are better, when we have more, when things change. And that new car may, in fact, make us happy for a time, but then we are likely to return to our old patterns of dissatisfaction.

In fact, happiness is an attitude, not a circumstance. The core of Mindfulness is this: BE HAPPY NOW! Nothing is required for happiness except a state of mind. Truly. It is a choice we make now.

Pay attention to your thoughts. Are you thinking about how unhappy you are, about all the problems you have? Ask yourself this: This very moment, right now, do I actually have a problem or am I really worrying about how my situations may cause me problems in the future? Right now, this very moment, as I take in this breath, I do not have a problem.

> *"Happiness is now or not at all."* Eckhart Tolle, author of *Power of Now*

Think about Tolle's statement. I can't be happy in the past; the past is gone. The future is not yet here; I can't be happy there. I can only be happy right now, in this moment. I can choose to be happy right now, with things just as they are.

Will there ever be a perfect moment, with no problems? Well, yes, actually. This moment is perfect, this one right now, when I simply go deeply into it and allow myself to love it with a joyous, open heart.

Intuition

Your morning practices are critical to opening your intuition. They are a way of asking the Universe to come out and play.

And then, throughout the day, focus on your intuitive senses, to develop your intuitive abilities further and to utilize them in very practical ways in making the critical decisions of your life.

Intuition is a completely natural gift that we all share. You use your natural gift of intuition all the time:

- You sense how others feel about each other.
- You sense the tension when you walk into a room.
- You sometimes know who is calling just before the phone rings.
- You check on the baby just in time.
- You open the book right to the answer you are seeking.
- You say, "I knew I shouldn't have done that!"
- You get chills or tears when someone expresses a deep truth.

Intuition is built into our language, when we say we are following a hunch or refer to women's intuition, or a gut instinct. Everyone, to some extent, is "psychic" and uses

"ESP." Just because science hasn't figured out how to explain it yet, doesn't mean that it isn't true.

> *"All truth passes through three stages. First, it is ridiculed. Second, it is violently opposed. Third, it is accepted as being self-evident."* Arthur Schopenhauer, German Philosopher

Think of television as a metaphor. Imagine a field, full of things you can't see, hear or feel, like television waves. This field is within Ataquay and it contains everything that was, is and is likely to be. And you can learn to tune in, like turning on the TV and selecting a channel.

I first understood about intuitive senses by reading *You Are Psychic!* by Pete Sanders. The principles he lays out have held up very well for me and remain the cornerstones of my understanding of intuition. Most of what I explain below, I first learned from Sanders' book, then worked with and expanded on for many years. To explore this topic more deeply, I highly recommend his book.

Your Intuitive Senses

You can learn to enhance and focus your intuition, calling it forth when you need it:

- for professional and financial success

- for greater understanding of yourself
- to enhance relationships and resolve conflicts
- to get guidance in difficult situations.

There are a number of ways that we can receive intuitive information. You might think of them as intuitive senses, including:

- Feeling
- Knowing
- Seeing in the mind's eye or dreams
- Seeing physical energy
- Hearing words and voices.

You have all of the intuitive senses but are probably strongest in one or two. Like the physical senses, some people have fairly normal intuitive senses and some have exceptional abilities. Although you can learn to strengthen all of your intuitive senses, the best approach is to focus on developing your strongest intuitive senses first. This will help you overcome your doubts about whether you are intuitive.

As you work with intuition, be patient and use a light touch. Intuitive senses are a bit like animals in the forest. Once in a while, they crash right into the clearing and get your immediate attention. But most of the time, we aren't even consciously aware that they are there. We need to be still and invite them to approach. If we get aggressive or pushy, if we chase after them, they run away.

The Intuitive Sense of Feeling

If you are a strong intuitive Feeler:

- You can usually sense when something is troubling others and want to help; you try to put them at their ease.
- When you say, "This doesn't feel right," you mean it literally.
- You must be comfortable: with people, with decisions, with places, with clothes.
- You are relatively unconcerned about time and deadlines.
- Many of your negative feelings—tension, depression, anxiety—may not be yours at all; you may have picked them up from someone else.
- Awareness that you often pick up the feelings of others may help prevent you from being overwhelmed.

To a Feeler, your entire body is a feeling reception area, but your solar plexus is the master antenna. To increase your intuitive feeling abilities, relax and breathe, close your eyes and gently focus your awareness on your solar plexus, imagining information flowing into you there. As always, use a light touch; don't force, push or try.

You probably already do this naturally: you turn toward objects or people you want to sense fully; you cross your arms over your solar plexus when you are uncomfortable or vulnerable and do not want to receive the energy coming your way.

If you are a strong Feeler, see if you can learn to differentiate between what you actually feel and feelings you are picking up from others. Just ask yourself the question and it will increase your awareness. If you realize you are picking up feelings from others that you do not want, see if it helps you to turn sideways or go behind a desk or other barrier to protect your solar plexus. If this is not possible, picture their feelings just passing through you without affecting your own emotional center.

To practice using your intuitive sense of feeling:

- Consciously feel rooms as you enter them.
- When you shake someone's hand, ask yourself how they feel to you.
- Take objects into your hands and feel their energy. Metal holds energy well; try holding someone else's ring and see what comes to you.

- Run your hands over objects or down lists when you are choosing; see which items activate your sense of feeling.

The Intuitive Sense of Knowing

If you are a strong intuitive Knower:

- Your mind works quickly and you bore easily.
- You finish others' sentences because you really do know what they are going to say
- You have flashes of insight.
- You multi-task easily and just naturally know which task needs your attention right now.
- You say, "I just know this is the right decision."
- You trust your inner knowing more than any planning or analysis.

Since impressions may be fleeting and have no other supporting information, this may be the hardest intuitive sense to trust initially. I have met Knowers who thought they weren't intuitive at all, because they didn't recognize this as a legitimate intuitive sense.

To enhance intuitive knowing, relax and breathe, close your eyes and gently focus your attention on the top of your head, imagining information flowing into you there. Be open to whatever comes. Don't force or try. Capture your very first impression; don't analyze and edit.

Knowing is an excellent intuitive sense for predicting the future, but remember that the future is not fixed; it is moving, it is changeable. Knowing what direction things are heading now gives you the opportunity to make a change or prepare for what seems likely.

To practice using your intuitive sense of knowing:

- Bring to mind an upcoming decision you must make or problem you need to resolve.
- Make a brief list of your possible options.
- One at a time, review each option, shifting your attention to your Knowing receptor at the top of your head.
- Jot down the very first impression you receive with each option.

The sense of knowing is so quick, that you may receive your knowing when you write each item on the list, making it unnecessary to go back over the list. That's how it normally happens to me: by the time I finish making the list, I know which option is best for me.

The Intuitive Sense of Hearing

If you are a strong intuitive Listener:

- You talk to yourself and probably get silent answers in

your mind that you may not even be aware of.

- You sometimes hear your name called inside your mind.
- You may hear a song in your mind that gives you insights or answers.
- You want to understand things thoroughly and will ask questions until you do.
- You want things to be logical, direct and clear.
- You may occasionally receive a warning or direction in a strong inner voice, like "Check on the baby now!"

A strong Intuitive Listener may think that what they hear is just their own thinking, logically working things out with questions and answers. They may not realize that their rational thinking is intertwined with intuitive information.

If you have trouble differentiating between your thoughts and your Intuitive Hearing, see if you can sense the location in your head. When I first started channeling Quado, and was working to keep my reception clear of my mental editing and questioning, I used the location of the thought as a primary guide. When Quado spoke, I sensed that the words were right in the center top of my head, like a seam between the halves of my brain, whereas other thinking and visualizing seemed to be on one side or the other.

To practice using your intuitive sense of hearing, here are two exercises:

- Every morning, as part of your morning practice, breathe down to a quiet place and ask for a word for the day. Write down the very first thing that comes, even if it doesn't make sense at that moment.
- As you become more comfortable with your word, begin to ask: Is there a message for me? Again, capture the very first thing.
- When you have a choice to make or a problem to be solved, ask an open-ended question: How shall I handle this? As always, write down the answer without editing or questioning.
- When you are about to meet with someone, just 10-15 minutes before the meeting, ask an open question: How shall I approach this person? Capture the first impression.

The Intuitive Sense of Seeing

If you are a strong intuitive seer:

- You receive insight via dreams or symbols.
- You may see energy patterns, like auras, with eyes open.
- You are good at spatial relationships.
- You want to see the whole picture and have time to formulate an integrated plan.

- Decisions are clearer when you can physically see the choices.
- You love light, windows, views.

There are two types of intuitive seeing:

- seeing energy and visions with your eyes open, including auras, colors and light, perhaps symbols or letters
- seeing visions and dreams in your inner vision.

My own personal experience is that I am strong in inner vision, but not a natural in seeing energy with my eyes open. I can see auras if I practice, but it is not the natural gift with me that it is for some. I do have one interesting example, however, of seeing energy.

One day, on a normal shopping trip, I pulled into a parking lot and got out of the car. I looked down at the car key and saw a very odd energy glow across the top. This particular car key had two parts, with a plastic top over the metal key. The glow was right where the plastic and the metal met. Because I didn't recognize this glow as an intuitive hint, I just put my keys in my purse and went shopping.

When I returned to the car, I pulled out the key. The top part was attached to my keyring, but the bottom part wasn't there; it had broken away. Luckily, the bottom part was on the ground, right next to the car. I conclude from this, that a certain energy is exuded by things that are about to break, an energy that can be seen by those attuned to it.

To enhance intuitive seeing, relax and breathe, close your eyes and gently focus your attention on your "third eye," a spot between your eyebrows and slightly above; imagine information flowing into you there.

When you wish to practice seeing energy, you will find that dim indoor light against a solid background is best; bright light and busy patterns make it hard to differentiate the subtle energy.

Here's a good first exercise in seeing energy:

- Find a place with somewhat dim indoor light.
- Breathe and relax, with your physical eyes open, and consciously and gently focus attention on your third eye as well.
- Hold your index fingers about 6 inches in front of your eyes, pointing at each other and almost touching.
- Relax your eyes, allowing them to slightly unfocus.
- Slowly pull the fingers apart and observe the band of energy that stretches between them. To me, this energy has a slightly greenish tinge.
- Have fun observing the energy as you move your fingers apart and together.

To practice seeing auras:

- Find a place with somewhat dim indoor light. Have a friend stand or sit in front of a wall with a solid color; ask them to relax.
- Breathe and relax, with your physical eyes open, and consciously and gently focus attention on your third eye as well.
- Look just beyond or to the side of your friend's head, using your peripheral vision only.
- Look for a subtle halo of energy around their head.
- Notice that when you look directly at them, the aura may disappear; return to peripheral vision and it reappears.
- As you practice more, you may see colors.

When you practice looking at auras, it is fun to do it with several people. Some will be natural aura spotters and their delight will be infectious and help others relax and overcome their hesitancy and skepticism. If you are a natural with this, you might want to explore the many books written to help you interpret aura colors.

As for inner visions, you may find, as I do, that there is a visual difference between normal visualizing and receiving an intuitive answer. For me, my intentional visualizing is sharper than a picture I receive as a result of asking a question. A picture I receive is often grainy.

I also find that my intuitive inner vision comes in conjunction with my intuitive hearing. When I am channeling, I will also see a picture in my mind that corresponds with the words I am hearing.

Striking Gold

There is another important intuitive sense that seems to work in conjunction with the others: when chills and/or tears signal that you have struck gold and touched a deep and important truth.

When I am channeling a message for someone, I will have a visual experience as well as receiving and conveying words of guidance and truth, and then I will suddenly say one thing that is so true and important that I get chills. If it is deeply emotional and involving love, it may also bring tears to my eyes. When this happens, it is always the most critical thing that needs to be known.

This is, of course, the state of Lhamata, that signals a deep connection into Ataquay. You may have experienced it when an artist is performing from deep within the heart of Ataquay or perhaps as an artist yourself, when you strike a deeply resonating truth or emotion.

Using Your Intuitive Senses Together

You are probably strongest in one or two of these senses and may use all of them in combination in normal life. Experiment with all of the intuitive senses to find your strengths and then focus on developing and using your strengths. Use your two strongest senses to cross-validate impressions. Keep an intuition journal to note your intuitive impressions and how they worked out.

> *"The intuitive mind is a sacred gift and the rational mind is a faithful servant. We have created a society that honors the servant and has forgotten the gift."*
> Albert Einstein

Keep practicing and you will develop more and more ways to impact your everyday life with amazing, accurate information.

The Well of Joy

In the next section, I focus on tools and techniques to influence your future. I think it is so much fun to explore these ideas and see what it may all mean, to play with intentional thought and action. I'm just so intrigued by it all!

To tell the truth, though, I may really be happiest when I choose to just love my life, exactly as it is, filled with gratitude for the wonderful little beauties and wonders around me. When I go for a walk, notice the fluffy clouds and hear the birds, I feel such joy, no matter what my life circumstances.

Honestly, it's hard to come up with a reason why I shouldn't just live that way, experiencing life as it unfolds and deeply embracing each moment, just as it is. And after all, do I really need to be thinking about what I want all the time? I suspect the Universe already knows.

And even when things are other than I desired, I know that deep in my center, there is a well of joy. It has nothing to do with my life circumstances or whether I got what I thought I wanted. It is just there, no matter what is happening in my life. And when I focus on this well of joy, it bubbles up and rises to meet my heart, lifting me and reminding me of the great blessings of simply being alive.

I know this sounds odd, even impossible, but it is absolutely true: I find that it is possible to tap into my well of joy to sustain me, even when the worst has happened, even when I am in the throes of grief. When my heart is breaking and I don't know quite how I can go on, if I turn my attention to it for just a moment, I am aware that the well is still full, waiting for me to return to it.

I believe, in fact I know, that you have that very same well of joy in your center. Drop down out of your busy mind and into your solar plexus, breathe and go deep and see if you can find that warm, bubbling, golden glow.

Ah, there it is. And here, within this golden well of peace, love and joy, is everything I need to live a beautiful life, one that is brand new and beautiful in every moment, now and now.

14 Building a Vibrant Future

This section focuses on tools and techniques that may help you influence the Universe in creating a desirable future.

Scary Good

Walking our Path of Destiny requires us to continually challenge ourselves to lift up to the next level, to take a deep breath of courage and step out and up. The Universe will often bring you opportunities that lead toward what you want, sometimes magically, but then you need to act with courage to take advantage of them.

> *"The cave you fear to enter holds the treasure you seek."* Joseph Campbell, author of *Hero with a Thousand Faces*

> *"Life begins at the end of your comfort zone."* Neale Donald Walsch, author of *Conversations with God*

I have found that the very best things in life come to us when we are in a state I call Scary Good. The Scary Good condition is when you know that you are meant to do something, that it is the right thing, that it is on your path, but you find it very scary. Examples that come to mind are: speaking to a stranger; asking for a favor; giving a talk; going on an audition; going to a job interview; making a sales call; speaking your truth, especially when it goes against the majority opinion; challenging power and authority; violating the norms of your family or society.

If you are stuck and need to get your life moving, locate the thing you are afraid of that is blocking you from moving forward and just do it. Remember that when you act, you always move forward, either because you succeeded or because you learned something about what to do better next time. If you don't act, you stay locked in fear and stasis.

Below are some tools that may help you do that Scary Good thing you want and need to do.

Heaven and Earth

This is a quick and easy energy exercise to help you center yourself.

- Stand and close or lower your eyes.
- Breathe deeply 3 times.
- See a golden column of light reaching down to you from the heavens.
- Feel the light flowing all the way through you and down into the center of the earth.
- Feel how your body relaxes.
- If you like, raise your chin and lift your arms up toward the light.
- See how your own center lights up with truth and power.
- Feel your own light and power expand outward as you glow with everything you are.
- Give thanks for being the strong, courageous and powerful person you truly are.

Luminous Egg

This technique is useful when you're tired, anxious or scattered and just not up to the task at hand. It is also very useful when you are dealing with difficult people or manipulative people who tend to steal your energy instead of generating their own.

If you like, you can do Heaven and Earth first to center yourself and then follow up with Luminous Egg.

The purpose of this exercise is to restore the integrity of your energy boundary. That boundary is shaped like a large egg and is transparent and luminous. You are standing in the middle of it. When you are tense, your egg will be just an inch or two out from the top of your head. When you are relaxed and feeling powerful, it will be further out, perhaps a foot or two.

Think of your energy boundary like the glass on a light bulb: the glass helps hold the energy in so that the light can shine brightly.

Sometimes your boundary gets damaged and energy leaks out. This exercise will repair the surface and allow you to hold your own energy in:

- Stand and close or lower your eyes.
- Breathe deeply 3 times.
- See yourself standing in the center of a big egg-shaped enclosure, clear and luminous. It is the boundary of your energy field.
- Focus on your heart and fill it with light and love. Watch as that light grows brighter and brighter.
- Send up a fountain of love from your heart, up through the top of your head until it reaches the egg.
- Let the love sheet down the outside of your boundary, like water pouring down the outside of an egg. As it

goes down, it is repairing all the little cracks and fissures, making it whole and smooth.

- When the love reaches the bottom of the egg, tuck it in under your feet.
- In the area between your knees and feet, see if there are any hooks that others have thrown into your field, that are causing your energy to drain. If so, just reach down, grab them and toss them away.
- Repeat sending up a fountain of love until you feel that your boundary is repaired.
- Then watch as your heart fills up your egg with love.
- Watch as your glow of love is so bright, that the love and light reach out, far beyond you. Know that, at some level, others will sense your secure and loving glow.

Don't concern yourself about the people whose hooks you have removed. Your job is to keep your own energy strong, not to allow others to drain you. Think of yourself as a torch: you are happy to glow and help light others, but you do not give away the fuel that keeps you burning. In fact, your job is to continually refresh that fuel and keep glowing for yourself and others.

One more comment about people who drain your energy, expecting you to make them happy. In the end they will be angry and disappointed with you, no matter how hard you try. Why? Because you will fail. Why? Because it is not possible to make another person happy, except for a temporary moment when you somehow manage to successfully fulfil a desire. In the end, happiness is an attitude and a choice we each can make; no one else can do that for us.

Power Posing

Amy Cuddy, a behavioral scientist at Harvard, gave a Ted talk on Power Posing. You may use the QR Code below to watch it.

Cuddy's researchers found that when you pose your body like a confident winner, arms out, chin up, chest high, that your body responds by increasing testosterone and decreasing cortisol, thus making you calmer (less cortisol) and more confident (more testosterone). Conversely, when you pose your body like someone defeated and timid, chest pulled in, chin down, eyes lowered, arms hugging your body, your body responds by decreasing testosterone and increasing cortisol, thus making you less confident and more anxious.

Cuddy said that you only have to hold a power pose for 2 minutes to have this effect on your physical body. I have found this technique to work, and I have also added two more elements to make it even more effective: Checking in and Power Animal power-up.

Do this 10-15 minutes before you do the Scary Good thing you know you truly want to do. You can do this at home alone earlier, but it is important to check in again just before you act, because things change. I have found that a bathroom stall or a car will do nicely as the last check-in.

Here are the steps:

- Take your 3 deep breaths into a relaxed state. This is why you've been practicing every morning, to make it easy to reach this place when you need to.
- Check in by asking: How shall I approach this (the Scary Good thing you are about to do)?
- Note the very first answer that occurs to you. It may be something like "act very confident" or "just be relaxed and friendly." It may also be something surprising.
- Think of an animal that embodies the characteristics you need, like a confident lion or lioness, a patient panther, a clever fox, an elephant who remembers

everything, a lovable Labrador. This will be your Power Animal in the following steps.

- Get into a power pose, perhaps lifting your arms like a winner crossing the finish line, or hands on hips like Wonder Woman. Begin your 2 minutes.
- Picture the Power Animal and invite him or her to join you, to be with you energetically. If you are able to, you may even growl and claw the air like the lion you truly are, fully embodying that Power Animal energy.
- Now breathe deeply again and just go do that Scary Good thing. And bring your Power Animal along with you.

I explain more about Power Animals later in the Toolkit.

The Rainbow of Love

If you are struggling with relationships, with family, coworkers or friends, you can improve the relationships by sending them a rainbow of love. Have your journal nearby.

- Breathe down to a relaxed state.
- State your intention for that specific person: "My intention is to establish a good relationship with [her name]."
- Close your eyes and picture the person.

- Take a deep breath and fill your heart with love.
- Connect with her by sending a rainbow of love from your heart to hers.
- If she is a challenging person, remember that you are connecting not just with her human personality, but also with her Aiyama, or higher self. Find some level where she is open to receiving your love.
- Write down any impressions you receive.

You may simply stop here, knowing that at some level, she will feel the loving connection. If you do this every day, your relationship will improve; just be patient. The Universe is also likely to get involved in helping you find ways to connect.

If this is an important relationship with serious issues, take it a step further, calling upon your intuition to give you answers. Do this at home, alone, in your quiet time for each person concerned:

- First, send the Rainbow of Love, as described above.
- Make sure you are all the way into Lhamata, a buzzy feeling you will come to recognize as you practice. Breathing Down is an excellent way to get there.
- When you feel connected, ask a few questions and jot down the very first thing that comes into your mind as an answer, even if it doesn't make sense to you right then. Note not only the words that came to you, but

also your feelings, knowings, images and symbols that show up. It is *so important* to capture the first impression, quite probably just a few words, before your analytical mind steps in and tries to make sense of it.

- Ask questions like these, always open-ended, never yes-no, and write down the answers: What does she want from me? How does she view me? What would it take for me to influence that view? What does she truly care about? What is she afraid of?
- Remember to ask what is often the most important question: How should I approach this person?
- Capture that answer just as it comes. Then act on it, if action is recommended.

You may receive your answers in words, as I do. But you may also receive it in an inner vision, or a feeling, or a flash of knowing. Write it down; describe what comes to you. If it doesn't make sense now, it will probably make sense later.

If you repeat the Rainbow of Love every day, it will get easier and easier to tune into this person. And then, it is likely that the Universe will jump in and start to give you the answers you need in other ways as well. Perhaps you will overhear a conversation that tells you what you need to do. Perhaps it will be an article that catches your attention or a TV show that discusses your issue. Perhaps you will run into the person and have an opportunity to heal the situation. Perhaps the answer will be to do nothing and to move on or wait.

Then, just before you initiate contact, either individually or in a group, you need to touch base again. This will get easier and easier, if you have already tuned in. You need to check in within 10-15 of the planned contact, to see if things have changed. For example, it might be that even though someone wants you to approach them, right now is a really bad time to call. Or, you might have a wonderful presentation prepared, but when you check in just before meeting, you learn that the timing is bad because of an urgent topic that just came up.

Here's an example of what happened to me. I was working for a woman, Linda, with whom I would meet weekly. I often intentionally connected with her in the morning, sending Rainbows, and I always checked in just before we met. One week, I had spent quite a bit of time preparing a lengthy agenda of all the things I wanted to cover. Then, 10 minutes before the meeting, I took a few deep breaths and asked: "How shall I approach Linda?"

The answer came flashing right back: "She is very busy. Pick one topic, that's all."

So I deleted all but one topic from my agenda and went off to her office.

I walked in and she said: "Oh, Carrie, I was just trying to call you to cancel our meeting. I just don't have time today."

I said: "I only have one quick topic." She responded, "Oh, in that case, all right. Come on in."

Helpers in Ataquay: Power Animals

There are many helpers in Ataquay, including angels and various types of spiritual guides and entities, like Quado and Running Wolf. When you spend time in Ataquay, they will come to you. Many books have been written about helpers, especially angels. I would encourage you to open to the form that seems to want to be with you.

I would like here to talk about somewhat lesser-known helpers, Power Animals, who can add a wonderful dimension to your life.

After years of working with Power Animals, I have come to understand them in a way that is not exactly the meaning held by the medicine man or shaman of old, who believed that a Power Animal had once been alive and was now lending you its health and vigor in order to live again through you.

Instead, I think of them as pure packets of intense, focused energy, energy that you can utilize in your life in very positive ways. Also, my pantheon of Power Animals is global, potentially containing any animal who lives or lived upon the earth, on any continent, in any sea. And going even further, it includes animals of myth, like unicorns, winged horses and dragons.

I also believe that with focus, concentration and practice, anyone can learn to access this power on their own, without requiring an intermediary like a shaman.

There are several ways to work with the powerful energy of the Power Animal. Below I explain two of the primary means: Generic and Specific.

Generic Power Animals

Humans have long associated animals with certain characteristics, for example, putting Lion on the coat of arms to show courage and confidence or Eagle to demonstrate soaring freedom, power and leadership. At the Generic Level, we are asking a Power Animal to give us the gift of its characteristics, the ones you just naturally associate with that animal.

You can develop your own personal ritual to bring in this energy and use it before important occasions, such as an important meeting. I have found it particularly effective to combine Power Animals and Power Posing, as I discussed earlier, holding your body in a powerful testosterone-elevating pose for 2 minutes while you picture the Power Animal that has the characteristics you desire.

At the Generic Level, you may choose the Power Animal you work with. You might call in Cougar to help you get healthy and fit, Swan to give you the gift of grace, Leopard to let you blend in and disappear or Panther to give you patience as you wait for the right opportunity to come down the path. Just choose the Power Animal that feels right to you and invite it to empower you.

Personal Power Animals

The Personal Level takes you into a relationship with a specific Power Animal, a relationship that may be for a transitional period, for a new phase of life or for a lifetime. At the Personal Level, you work with and are guided not only by Lion or Panther, but by a specific Lion or Panther, one who has a name and a personality, one that you might be able to see in your mind's eye, one who probably speaks to you with guidance, one who is a loving companion and makes you feel warm, safe and secure.

You may already know who your primary personal Power Animal is. He or she may have come to you in a dream, or shown up often in physical form outside your window or simply appeared in your mind's eye, standing by and ready to work with you.

You might meet your Power Animal on my website, PowerAnimalsUnleashed.com, where you will go into the

Enchanted Forest and allow your intuition to tell you when to click and bring forth your new companion. Just use the QR Code below.

Or you can use the traditional method by going to the Land of the Power Animals to retrieve a Power Animal who wishes to be with you, led either by a shaman or simply by listening to a recording of shaman drumming and allowing your intuitive mind to guide you.

You begin by going down into the earth in your mind's eye, perhaps sliding down a tree root or, as I do, going into a cave and jumping into a pool of water. It is then like going down a rabbit hole, twisting and turning, and you finally emerge in a landscape—perhaps Africa, perhaps in a jungle, perhaps even under water.

You travel through that landscape until an animal presents itself to you in four aspects, usually front, back, side and side. This is its signal that it wishes to be with you. This animal knows you, your circumstances and what you need in order to successfully navigate what lies ahead. It is asking to be your companion, helper and guide for this time in your life, your personal Power Animal. If you agree, you reach out and pull the Power Animal close.

If you like, you may call to Running Wolf and ask him to perform a ceremony to join you to your Power Animal energetically.

It is then up to you to build your relationship with your Power Animal. Ask for a name and one will flash in your mind. Do what pleases your Power Animal, like taking long walks in the forest. Find out how your Power Animal wants to communicate with you. Ask questions and learn how the answers will come: perhaps in words that you capture in a journal, perhaps in visions or a flash of knowing, perhaps in a feeling in your heart. Work with your Power Animal as a guide and a companion. Follow the advice and keep a journal of the advice and the results.

As you work with your Power Animal, begin to feel and understand the increased power that is now yours. Call your Power Animal into your energetic field whenever you interface with people, especially in difficult circumstances and relationships. Notice if you become healthier and more vibrant, more confident and courageous. Notice if your relationships improve.

I had one client with a very demanding corporate job. When she went into a meeting, she always tried to have an empty chair beside her, a place for her Wolf, Luthor, to take his seat at the table.

Remember, too, that you can work with more than one Power Animal. If another one comes to you, in a vision or a dream, feel free to accept its help in addition to your primary Power Animal. You might also have specific Power Animals for different parts of your life. For example, you might have a Power Animal that helps you with your Reiki practice and a different one who helps you with personal relationships or life in general.

Generic and Personal Together

Feel free to add the occasional Generic Power Animal to your life, even as you work with your Personal Power Animals. For example, suppose that your primary Power Animal, the one you work with every day, is an Owl, who brings you great wisdom. But now, you are going into a potentially confrontational meeting in which you need confidence and courage. Feel free to call in Lion to help you with the meeting. Owl will not be offended.

My Power Animal was Panther for most of my life. As a child, when we played jungle animals, I was always Panther. Panther energy watches and waits for the time to be right to act. Tiger, who has a lot of very directed energy, helped me build the PowerAnimalsUnleashed.com website. Lion also worked with me when I was beginning to develop a business for Ed's book and products, because he was Ed's Power Animal. It seems that the big cats were always with me, in various ventures.

But more recently, a very different Power Animal came to me at a most critical moment. The day after Ed died, Elephant came to me, just showing up in my mind, offering to give me the strength to do what I needed to do and then guiding me to be with family, taking me home to heal.

Participating with the Universe

Building a vibrant future means establishing a relationship with the Universe in which you are participating together in lively interaction.

The key words for full participation with the Universe are:

Attitude
Acceptance
Attention
Intention
Action.

Attitude

There is a way to interact with the universe that involves holding two loosely-opposing thoughts as your truth at one and the same time, thereby creating a beautiful attitude of wonder, curiosity, surprise, gratitude and graceful acceptance. This attitude not only feels wonderful, peaceful and blissful inside, but also appears to be highly acceptable to the universe, inviting it to play and dance alongside you, bringing surprising gifts at every turn.

I experience all of this as true:

- I am unique and individual in all the universe, while at the same time, I am one with all that is. I am a unique wave, yet also experience myself as the vast and infinite ocean itself.
- My life may seem affected by forces outside of me, yet I feel and know myself as everywhere and everything. There are times when I focus on trimming my sails to the prevailing winds, yet I also know myself as being the wind itself.
- My physical body is decaying and will eventually turn to dust, yet I know myself as immortal. This human lifetime is like the rose that blooms for its season, sending its perfume across the garden, yet eventually falls to the ground and becomes the soil that feeds the roots of the plant itself.

- I am deeply aware and immensely powerful, an energy force beyond reckoning, yet I am also humble, having no expectation of control, or even of full understanding, of the forces at work in the universe and how they may affect my human experience. Sometimes I am powerful like an elephant, the earth shaking as I pass; at other times my power is that of a delicate butterfly who only senses and lightly responds.

If you can manage to walk on the edge, balancing uniqueness with wholeness, individuality with oneness, mortality with immortality, power with vulnerability, life will reward you in countless, yet indescribable, ways.

Acceptance

Acceptance is a simple recognition of what exists at this moment, even when you fully intend to do everything you can to change it. Your intentions and actions will always be more effective if you begin with acknowledgement of what is, rather than coming from resistance or denial.

> *"What you resist not only persists, but will grow in size."* Carl Jung, Psychologist

> *"Accept—then act. Whatever the present moment contains, accept it as if you had chosen it. Always work with it, not against it."* Eckhart Tolle, author of *Power of Now*

Attention

Attention and Intention refer to your interaction with the Universe. I think of Attention as receiving and Intention as sending.

Receiving is paying careful attention to guidance, signs and signals coming your way in order to attune yourself to the ever-changing environment in which you live and take advantage of opportunities that are continually opening around you. Developing your intuitive senses, as discussed in the previous Centering into the Present section, is the best possible way to take advantage of the information, guidance and assistance that is flowing your way.

> *"Whatever you put your attention on will grow stronger in your life."* Deepak Chopra, author of *Book of Secrets*

I also have a method of receiving guidance when I make choices between multiple options. I picture the choices as divergent paths in the woods, as follows:

- Have pencil and paper handy.
- Close your eyes and visualize several paths that go through the woods, one path for each choice you might make.
- Clearly name the choices and paths. You may wish to designate one path as "no action at this time."
- Take a deep breath and engage all your intuitive senses, opening the top of your head for knowing, your third eye for seeing, your ears for hearing and your solar plexus for feeling.
- Experience each path in turn. How do you feel when you observe it? Is it bright or dark? Do any words come to you? Is it light or heavy? Is it long or short? Does it slant upwards or down?
- Write down your impression of the path, just as it comes to you, without analysis or editing.
- When you are done with all the paths, review what has come to you. Normally, you will have a lot of clear intuitive information about each choice.

When you have an important choice to make, feel free to ask other intuitive people to join you in this exercise. Go through all of the paths together, each person noting their own impressions. Then, when all the paths are complete, compare notes. This is not only fun, but it serves to validate your findings when everyone comes to the same conclusion independently.

I have another method for choosing that is more kinesthetic. I hold my hands out to the side as I focus on an action I might take and ask: shall I do this? If the answer is yes, one of my hands lifts up; if I absolutely should do it, my hand will shoot up high. If it is a definite no, the hand drops. If it is a maybe, the hands stay still.

Then I focus on the next possible action.

The guidance of "maybe" can also be expressed as "do it if you want to." From years of experience, I can say that an intuitive "maybe" is best treated as a no. It means that nothing horrible will happen if you do it, but neither will anything positive occur that moves you forward. It usually means you will simply be wasting your time or money.

Intention

Intention is the act of letting the Universe (and yourself, of course, since you are the Universe) know the life you wish to create and the type of opportunities you would like to move into. Many people have developed processes to harness your energetic power to make your dreams come true, variously known as manifestation, spontaneous wish fulfillment or intention mastery.

I suspect you can choose whatever method you like, since in the end, they all involve ways to focus your attention toward what you wish to create. And I do believe that being clear about what you want in life is immensely useful and effective, especially when you allow it to evolve as life moves forward. In fact, when I am in a period of confusion or transition, I often hear a voice in my head saying: "What do you want? Say what you want!"

As I mentioned earlier, I also have a little prayer of my own that I like to offer the Universe before I state any desires or intentions. I say: "I ask that my desires be completely congruent with the path I am here to walk." I simply no longer wish to go chasing after a desire of my ego that takes me away from a true, authentic direction.

All that said, I think it is worthwhile to take the time to define the life you wish to create and include it in your morning quiet time.

When you contemplate the life that you want to create, I find that it is useful to look at it in these categories:

Health

Wealth

Relationships

Creative self-expression

Meaningful work.

In fact, you can start right now by getting a nice journal of blank pages, writing today's date and then describing how you would like your life to be in each of these areas.

As you move forward, you will find that you not only build the knowledge and tools to create the life you want, but that the description of the life you want to create evolves along with your knowledge and skills. Allow this to happen. As you develop a new relationship with yourself and the Universe, as you begin to understand your own growing power, write down your new understandings of what you truly wish to create.

You will want to phrase your written statements in a way that is true for you and has the energy of planned action, not wishful daydreaming.

A good way is to begin with "I intend to" or "my intention is." For example: My intention is to be healthy and fit in all ways, to achieve a weight of 150 pounds and maintain it for the rest of my life.

Your goal is clarity, so the more specific you are, the better. Some people say it is important to specify desired timing, for example "to find a great job by September 30th." I have tried this, but it always felt a little uncomfortable to me.

Sometimes things just happen in their own time. I am also uncomfortable with stating intentions as being already true, although I know that some people teach this as the best way.

Deepak Chopra wrote *Spontaneous Fulfillment of Desire*, which explains his whole philosophy of how it all works. He suggests that you focus lightly on your intention before your daily meditation and then simply release it, letting the universe "handle the details." I like the ease and lightness of this approach.

Here are some observations from my own experience with intention:

- As is always true in working with intuition, use a light touch. Desperation and fear are not your friends when you speak to the Universe. Forcing, pushing and trying to control tend to drive away what you wish to bring forward. Not only that, but an overly-strong attachment to a specific outcome may lead into disappointment and depression if it doesn't work out quickly.
- Allow your desires and intentions to evolve. If you focus daily on your intentions, you may find that they shift and you come up with new intentions. Allow space for your intuition to give you feedback on your desires.

- If your Sending isn't working, then just let it go and shift back to Receiving for a while. After all, perhaps the Universe has a better idea than what you said you wanted and if you pay attention, you may see a better path.

Action

I have found this to be true: If I act, I will either succeed or I will learn something. If I don't act, then I may simply stay stuck or confused, wishing something would change or clarify.

Sometimes the best way to get the Universe to start creating opportunities is to simply stir things up by doing things you have never done before. Walk down a different street, go into a store you usually pass by, turn right instead of left, talk to strangers, say yes to invitations you would normally refuse, join a new group or class.

I have found that the Universe will deliver knowledge and opportunities, but if you don't act decisively to take advantage, they simply pass you by. One such example was a couple of stock tips I received some years ago. I was doing yoga when a voice in my head said: "Buy Microsoft." I kid you not. I followed this direction, but I invested only a small amount. The stock did well, very well, and of course, I wished I had invested far more. Then, a few years later, a voice said: "Sell Microsoft." I ignored this advice—the stock had done so well, I just couldn't let it go!—and watched as I lost much of what I had gained.

A few more interesting notes about my Microsoft experience. First, I had been paying attention to stocks and investing, so I had opened up that channel of information. Second, Microsoft was in my Web of connections, since Ed and I had discussed the company and once seriously considered applying for work with them. The company is also in the city of my birth and where my sister lives.

I think all this matters. Where you put your attention is a form of intention. And the Universe tends to deliver information and opportunities that are connected to you in some way.

Begin from where you are, taking the small steps right in front of you. Get ready for opportunities that may come, by having your skills developed and your resume, audition or demo prepared. Readiness is, in fact, a particularly potent form of Intention.

Then, take a deep breath and act with courage, remembering that it is through people that things actually happen. Go ahead and pick up the phone and call that agent. Do your streaming broadcast. Record your podcast and tell people about it. Learn new software. Ask people if they know of a great opportunity for you. Do that Scary Good thing that helps stretch you and lift you to the next level. And if you fall flat on your face the first time out, just do what the song says: pick yourself up, dust yourself off and start all over again.

Remember, too, to let your fears be your guide to what you need to tackle next.

You can do it. You can be it. Or you can at least give it your best shot and know that you did.

Bringing it Together

Here's a fun story of combining an open, positive Attitude with Attention, Intention and Action. It's such a lovely example of how the Web of the Universe loves to connect everything it possibly can, just clicking it all into place: click, click, click.

I had joined a Power of Eight class with Lynne McTaggart to learn to become a Master of Intention. One of my intentions, which I was repeating daily in a morning ritual, was this:

> "My intention, beginning now and continuing for the rest of my life, is to build a growing community of friends, who are intelligent, curious and interesting, who love music, wine and good conversation, who enjoy life, have a great sense of humor and laugh easily."

I flew to Phoenix to see an old friend. When I checked in for my flight 24 hours before, I had an opportunity to purchase an upgrade to First Class. I used my kinesthetic test: I held out my hands and asked my intuitive self: should I upgrade? My hand flew up; the answer was yes. So I did.

I got on the plane and sat down next to a woman named Cindy. Cindy had just upgraded one hour earlier. I mention this, because I find it interesting that neither of us were in the seats we originally ticketed.

I had asked the Universe for local friends. Cindy also lived in Palos Verdes, 5 minutes from my apartment. Click.

I had asked for friends who loved music. Cindy teaches the violin. Click.

And who does she teach? The youth orchestra started in Los Angeles by Gustavo Dudamel, the conductor of my great experience in singing Mahler with the Los Angeles Philharmonic. Click.

But, Cindy said, even though she teaches violin, her primary instrument is actually the bass. The bass, really? It just so happens I have a bass sitting in my living room, a present I had given Ed for his 75th birthday. Click.

When I got back home, I called Cindy and asked her to come over for coffee. She arrived at my house with two bows, to try out my bass. She told me she had two bows, because one of them she only used for Mahler. Click.

Remember that I asked for friends who enjoyed wine? Well, when she had me over to coffee at her house, she showed me her wine cellar. Click.

It also turned out we both had Subaru Outbacks, but by then it was clear that the universe was just showing off.

15 What Does It All Mean?

Some magical things feel as if they happen because they are an important step on my path, like the story I told earlier about how I got to sing in the Mahler concert with the Los Angeles Philharmonic. It felt fully orchestrated, including a prophetic vision years earlier.

On the other hand, I feel that the Cindy connection was the result of my conscious and deliberate intentions, but not something with deeper implications for my life. I had taken that class specifically to see if intentions can work and here was my answer: yes, they can.

I do believe that the Web of the Universe, with its driving desire to connect, is influenced by our thoughts, feelings and desires as well as our actions. But it's also clear to me that my attention and participation are required to complete the connections. For example, if I had decided that I shouldn't spend money to upgrade on such a short flight, I probably would not have met Cindy.

And yet the story of my house (Chapter 10, Embracing the Mystery), shows that no matter how much we want what we want, we will sometimes do best to listen and follow, surrendering to what is and trusting, hoping, that the Universe knows best.

We are in a dialogue, an interplay, with the Universe. We are not in charge and in control, but neither are we helpless. The Web, our Path, our attention, intentions and actions are all like the threads in an intricate and beautiful tapestry. And when we choose to do something Scary Good, it is like taking a stitch with a vibrant red thread, and the whole tapestry is changed.

And perhaps, someday, when this adventure is over and we return fully to Aiyama, we will get to see the whole amazing work of art.

16 READING LIST

Below are the books referenced in my book as well as a few others that I recommend, in sequence by the author's last name. Use the QR code below to go to a webpage with links to all of these books on amazon.

Radical Healing, by Rudolph Ballentine, M.D.

Steering by Starlight, by Martha Beck

Dare to Lead, by Brené Brown

The Artist's Way, A Spiritual Path to Higher Creativity, by Julia Cameron and Mark Bryan

The Hero with a Thousand Faces, by Joseph Campbell

Creating Affluence, by Deepak Chopra

The Book of Secrets, by Deepak Chopra

The Spontaneous Fulfillment of Desire, by Deepak Chopra

Big Magic, by Elizabeth Gilbert

The Art of Living, by Thich Nhat Hanh

The Way of the Shaman, by Michael Harner

Edisms Revealed, the Wit and Wisdom of Ed Hart, by Edward C. Hart, edited by Carrie Hart

Heal Your Body, by Louise L. Hay

The Power of Eight, by Lynne McTaggart

The Four Agreements, by Don Miguel Ruiz

You Are Psychic! by Pete Sanders

The Power of Now, by Eckhart Tolle

17 ABOUT THE AUTHOR

IN HER OWN WORDS

I was raised outside of any religion and spent my professional life as an IT manager and executive in corporate America, with no particular interest in anything mystical. Then, at 50 years old, the world of spirit and mystery came seeking me in the form of messages from Quado, a spiritual entity. Quado taught me the timeless principles that formed the foundation of my work. I shared the loving messages of Quado for over ten years, then moved on to other adventures, including working with Power Animals and Running Wolf, a shaman.

I then began work with Wanataquay, a new energy that came to me. Ataquay is a word from the language of Wanataquay, describing the place I love most in the world, the place where ordinary time and space give way to serendipity and coincidence, where we feel our way using our natural intuitive gifts, surrounded by help and love.

This book summarizes the very best of what I learned in over 25 years of exploration in Ataquay and the tools and techniques that helped me in the creation of a new life following the death of my husband of 46 years. I can't even imagine what it would have been like to survive that experience without the help and love that always surround me in Ataquay.

And now, I invite you to join me there, first to reach deep inner peace, greeting each dawn with joy and anticipation, then utilizing our amazing intuitive and creative gifts, shining out with our unique greatness and power, to create a better world for everyone.

If you would like to know what I am up to now, please join me on CarrieHart.com. Just use the QR Code below.

Made in USA - North Chelmsford, MA
1330567_9780966593174
09.06.2022 1738